The Book of the
FORD CORTINA, CORSAIR AND CLASSIC to 1970

The Corsair 2000E

The Cortina 1600E

The Pitman Motorists' Library

The Book of the
FORD CORTINA, CORSAIR AND CLASSIC to 1970

Maintenance and repair in the home garage for do-it-yourself owners

Staton Abbey, M.I.M.I.

Pitman Publishing

First published 1964
Second edition 1967
Third edition 1969
Reprinted 1971
Revised and reprinted 1973

SIR ISAAC PITMAN AND SONS LTD
Pitman House, Parker Street, Kingsway, London WC2B 5PB
P.O. Box 46038, Portal Street, Nairobi, Kenya

SIR ISAAC PITMAN (AUST.) PTY LTD
Pitman House, Bouverie Street, Carlton, Victoria 3053, Australia

PITMAN PUBLISHING COMPANY S.A. LTD
P.O. Box 11231, Johannesburg, South Africa

PITMAN PUBLISHING CORPORATION
6 East 43rd Street, New York, N.Y. 10017, U.S.A.

SIR ISAAC PITMAN (CANADA) LTD
495 Wellington Street West, Toronto 135, Canada

THE COPP CLARK PUBLISHING COMPANY
517 Wellington Street West, Toronto 135, Canada

ISBN: 0 273 42246 4

Text set in 8/9 pt Monotype Times New Roman, printed by letterpress,
and bound in Great Britain at The Pitman Press, Bath
G.4181:19

Preface

THIS book is intended for the do-it-yourself owner with a bent for "profitable tinkering"—and it *can* be profitable to the tune of perhaps £20 a year or more, if you do most of the work yourself, when labour charges can amount to £2 an hour or more in a large garage.

A good deal of ground which is outside the scope of the normal manufacturer's handbook is therefore covered. Jobs such as decarbonizing, ignition timing, carburettor adjustments, brake relining and similar work that can be done in the home garage, without the aid of special tools, for example, are described in detail.

For the benefit of the owner who is unable to obtain an instruction book for his car, however, it should be emphasized that normal routine maintenance and simple adjustments are fully dealt with. Moreover an attempt has been made to explain the whys and wherefores of the various jobs, instead of simply detailing what must be done, and when. The novice should therefore be able to tackle the work with confidence.

The information given has been carefully checked, but no liability can be accepted for any errors or omissions, or for changes in the specifications of the models covered by this book.

Grateful thanks are due to the Ford Motor Company for their assistance and co-operation when this book was being prepared. I shall always be glad to hear from readers, however, who may be able to pass on hints and suggestions based on their practical experience with these cars.

CREEK HOUSE   STATON ABBEY
ST. OSYTH
ESSEX

Contents

1 Getting to know your car

ALTHOUGH the figures and tables in this chapter may perhaps seem a little forbidding to the novice, more experienced owners will probably welcome as much detailed information as possible concerning their cars. Much of the data will, of course, be needed during routine servicing. Some of the facts are repeated in other chapters but they are included here for ease of reference. There is one point to bear in mind, however: car design is never static and modifications are often made during production of a particular model.

In this book we shall be dealing with three basic types of engine. The early range of Classic, Cortina and Corsair cars had in-line four-cylinder engines in which the carburettor and exhaust system were on the same side of the cylinder head. These may be termed in-line-port engines. In October 1967, the Cortina 1300 and 1600 were given cross-flow engines, with the carburettor and exhaust manifold on opposite sides of the head, and with the combustion chambers formed in the piston crowns instead of in the cylinder head. At the 1965 Motor Show a V4 engine was introduced for the Corsair. This was also of the cross-flow, bowl-in-piston type. We shall therefore be referring in this and subsequent chapters to *in-line-port*, *cross-flow* and *V4* engines.

RECOMMENDED LUBRICANTS

Use only reputable branded oils having viscosities specified below

Engine

Temperate climates	SAE 20 grade oil or 10W/30/40 multigrade
Above 90°F (or worn engine)	SAE 30 grade oil or 20W/50 multigrade
32°F to —10°F	SAE 10W grade oil
Below —10°F	SAE 10W plus 10% kerosene, or SAE 5W if available
Gearbox	SAE 80EP
Automatic transmission	Duckham's NOL automatic gear oil, BP Energol ATF-B fluid, Shell S6051, Regent 4571 Texamatic
Rear axle	SAE 90EP
Steering gearbox	SAE 90EP
Grease gun	Multipurpose grease with molybdenum disulphide or colloidal graphite additive
Brake and clutch fluid	Use only approved fluid supplied by Ford dealer

ENGINE SPECIFICATION

All models have four cylinders, arranged in line except for V4 engines, in which cylinders are in two banks at an included angle of 60°

Model	Bore	Stroke	Capacity	Compression Ratio (Standard)	(Optional)	Power Developed (Standard Comp. Ratio) at b.h.p.	at r.p.m.
Cortina 1200, up to October 1964 **Cortina 1200, October 1964–October 1970**	80·97 mm (3·19 in.)	58·17 mm (2·29 in.)	1,198 c.c. (73 cu in.)	8·7:1 9·1:1	7·3:1 7·8:1	48·5 50	4,800 4,900
Cortina, Corsair 1500, up to October 1964, Classic 1500 **Cortina, Corsair 1500, October 1964–October 1970**		72·75 mm (2·86 in.)	1,498 c.c. (91·4 cu in.)	8·3:1 9·0:1	7·0:1 7·5:1	59·5 61·5	4,600 4,700
Classic 1340		65·07 mm (2·56 in.)	1,340 c.c. (81·78 cu in.)	8·5:1	7·2:1	54	4,900
Cortina, Corsair 1500, G.T. models		72·75 mm (2·86 in.)	1,498 c.c. (91·4 cu in.)	9·0:1	—	78	5,200
Cortina 1300, October 1966–October 1967 **Cortina 1300, October 1967–October 1970**		62·99 mm (2·48 in.)	1,298 c.c. (79·2 cu in.)	9·0: 9·0:1	— 8·0:1	53·5 58	5,000 5,000
Cortina 1600 up to October 1970 **Cortina 1600 GT up to October 1970**		77·62 mm (3·06 in.)	1,599 c.c. (97·6 cu in.)	9·0:1 9·2:1	8·0:1 —	71 88	5,000 5,400
Corsair V4, 2000 V4	93·7 mm (3·69 in.)	60·4 mm (2·38 in.)	1,664 c.c. (101·5 cu in.)	9·1:1	7·7:1	81·5	4,750
Corsair V4 GT, 2000 de Luxe **Corsair 2000E**		72·4 mm (2·85 in.)	1,996 c.c. (121·8 cu in.)	8·9:1 8·9:1	7·7:1 —	93 97	4,750 5,000

Firing Order

V4 engines 1(R), 3(L), 4(L), 2(R)—(R and L, right-hand and left-hand side, as viewed from the driving seat
All in-line engines 1, 2, 4, 3

IGNITION SYSTEM

Type of system	12 volt oil-filled coil and distributor. Resistor type coil on later models (see page 73)

Ignition timing, B.T.D.C. (assuming the use of 97 octane, 4-star fuel—see also page 77)

Cortina 1200, Classic 1340	6°
Corsair, Cortina, Classic 1500	8°
Cortina 1300, up to October 1967	6°
Cortina 1300, October 1967 onwards	10°
Cortina 1600	10°
Cortina 1600 GT	8°
Corsair V4, 2000 V4 and V4 GT:	
High compression	8°
Low compression	4°
Corsair 2000 de Luxe and 2000E	10°

Contact-breaker points gap:

Lucas distributor	0·014—0·016 in.
Ford distributor	0·025 in.

Sparking plugs	Plug type	Gap
Classic, Cortina, Corsair 1500, in-line-port engines (up to October 1967)	Motorcraft AG 32	0·023 in.
Cortina 1300, 1600, 1600E, GT, cross-flow engines (from October 1967)	Motorcraft AG 22	0·025 in.
Corsair V4, V4 GT, 2000, 2000E	Motorcraft AG 22	0·025 in.

VALVE CLEARANCES

	Engine Hot		Engine Cold	
	Inlet	Exhaust	Inlet	Exhaust
All models except GT and Corsair V4	0·010 in.	0·017 in.	0·008 in.	0·018 in.
GT models except Corsair V4 GT	0·012 in.	0·022 in.	0·010 in.	0·023 in.
Corsair V4, V4 GT, 2000 and 2000E	0·010 in.	0·018 in.	0·012 in.	0·023 in.

CAPACITIES

	Engine (including filter)	Cooling System	Fuel Tank
Classic 1340	4½ Imp pints (5·4 U.S. pints, 2·56 litres)	10¾ Imp pints[1] (12·9 U.S. pints, 6·2 litres)	9 Imp gal (10·8 U.S. gal, 40·8 litres)
Classic 1500	6¾ Imp pints (8·1 U.S. pints, 3·9 litres)	10¾ Imp pints[1] (12·9 U.S. pints, 6·2 litres)	9 Imp gal (10·8 U.S. gal, 40·8 litres)
Cortina 1200 up to approx. December 1964	4½ Imp pints (5·4 U.S. pints, 2·56 litres)	9 Imp pints[1] (10·8 U.S. pints, 5·1 litres)	8 Imp gal (9·6 U.S. gal, 36 litres)
Cortina 1200 after approx. December 1964	5½ Imp pints (6·6 U.S. pints, 3·12 litres)	9 Imp pints[1] (10·8 U.S. pints, 5·1 litres)	8 Imp gal (9·6 U.S. gal, 36 litres)
Cortina 1500 and 1500 GT up to approx. December 1964	6½ Imp pints (7·7 U.S. pints, 3·7 litres)	10¾ Imp pints[1] (12·9 U.S. pints, 6·2 litres)	8 Imp gal (9·6 U.S. gal, 36 litres)
Cortina 1500 and 1500 GT after approx. December 1964	7 Imp pints (8·4 U.S. pints, 4·26 litres)	10¾ Imp pints[1] (12·9 U.S. pints, 6·2 litres)	8 Imp gal (9·6 U.S. gal, 36 litres)
Cotina 1300 up to October 1967	5½ Imp pints (6.6 U.S. pints, 3·12 litres)	10¼ Imp pints[2] (12·2 U.S. pints, 5·8 litres)	10 Imp gal (12 U.S. gal, 45·5 litres)
Cortina 1300 after October 1967	6½ Imp pints (7·7 U.S. pints, 3·7 litres)	10¼ Imp pints[2] (12·2 U.S. pints, 5·8 litres)	10 Imp gal (12 U.S. gal, 45·5 litres)
Cortina 1300 Estate from February to October 1967	5½ Imp pints (6·6 U.S. pints, 3·12 litres)	10¼ Imp pints[2] (12·2 U.S. pints, 5·8 litres)	8 Imp gal (9·6 U.S. gal, 36 litres)
Cortina 1300 Estate from October 1967	6½ Imp pints (7·7 U.S. pints, 3·7 litres)	10¼ Imp pints[2] (12·2 U.S. pints, 5·8 litres)	8 Imp gal (9·6 U.S. gal, 36 litres)
Cortina 1600 and 1600 GT	7¼ Imp pints (8·6 U.S. pints, 4·1 litres)	11½ Imp pints[2] (13·8 U.S. pints, 6·5 litres)	10 Imp gal (12 U.S. gal, 45·5 litres)
Cortina 1600 Estate	7¼ Imp pints (8·6 U.S. pints, 4·1 litres)	11½ Imp pints[2] (13·8 U.S. pints, 6·5 litres)	8 Imp gal (9·6 U.S. gal, 36 litres)
Corsair 1500	6½ Imp pints[3] (7·7 U.S. pints, 3·7 litres)	10¾ Imp pints[1] (12·9 U.S. pints, 6·2 litres)	8 Imp gal[3] (9·6 U.S. gal, 36 litres)
Corsair 1500 GT	6½ Imp pints[3] (7·7 U.S. pints, 3·7 litres)	11 Imp pints[1] (13·2 U.S. pints, 6·42 litres)	8 Imp gal[3] (9·6 U.S. gal, 36 litres)
Corsair V4, V4 de Luxe	7½ Imp pints (9 U.S. pints, 4·26 litres)	12½ Imp pints[1] (15 U.S. pints, 7·6 litres)	10 Imp gal (12 U.S. gal, 45·5 litres)
Corsair V4 GT, 2000 de Luxe, 2000E and Estate	7½ Imp pints (9 U.S. pints, 4·26 litres)	14 Imp pints[1] (16·8 U.S. pints, 7·9 litres)	10 Imp gal (12 U.S. gal, 45·5 litres)

[1] Allow 1–2 pints extra if heater is fitted
[2] Including heater
[3] Engine: 7½ Imp pints after April 1965
Fuel tank: 10 Imp gal on later models

TYRES

Saloons fitted with cross-ply tyres

When car is fully laden, increase rear tyre pressures by 4 lb/sq in. (0·28 kg/cm^2).
For driving at speeds exceeding 75 m.p.h. for more than one hour, increase all pressures by 4 lb/sq in. (0·28 kg/cm^2).

Estate cars fitted with cross-ply tyres

Fully laden, increase rear pressures by 9 lb/sq in. (0·63 kg/cm^2).
For continuous high speed increase front and rear pressures by 4 lb/sq in. (0·28 kg/cm^2).
Fully laden at high speed, increase front pressures by 4 lb/sq in. (0·28 kg/cm^2) and rear pressures by 9 lb/sq in. (0·63 kg/cm^2).

Saloons and estate cars fitted with radial-ply tyres

Do not increase standard pressures when fully loaded or for fast driving.

		Pressures			
		Front		*Rear*	
	Size	lb/sq in.	kg/cm^2	lb/sq in.	kg/cm^2
Cortina 1200	5·20–13	22	1·55	22	1·55
Cortina, Corsair 1500, Classic	5·60–13	22	1·55	24	1·7
Cortina GT up to October 1967	5·60–13	24	1·7	24	1·7
Cortina 1300 up to October 1967	5·20–13	24	1·7	24	1·7
Cortina 1300 from October 1967 and Cortina 1600	5·60–13	24	1·7	24	1·7
	165–13	24	1·7	28	2·0
Cortina 1600E	165–13	24	1·7	24	1·7
Cortina GT from October 1967	165–13	24	1·7	28	2·0
Corsair 1500 GT	5·60–13	24	1·7	26	1·8
Corsair V4	5·60–13	24	1·7	24	1·7
Corsair V4 GT	5·60–13	26	1·8	30	2·1
Corsair 2000, 2000E and Estate	165–13	24	1·7	30	2·1
Cortina Estate up to February 1967	6·00–13	22	1·55	30	2·1
Cortina Estate from February 1967	5·60–13	24	1·7	24	1·7
	165–13	24	1·7	28	2·0

DIMENSIONS AND WEIGHTS (APPROXIMATE)

	Overall Length	*Overall Width*	*Height*	*Turning Circle*	*Ground Clearance*	*Unladen Weight**
Cortina 1200, Cortina 1500 up to October 1966	14 ft 0 in. (4·27 m)	5 ft 2 in. (1·57 m)	4 ft 8½ in. (1·43 m)	35 ft (10·67 m)	6½ in. (16·51 cm)	15½–16¼ cwt (785–832 kg)
Cortina GT up to October 1966	14 ft 2 in. (4·33 m)	5 ft 2 in. (1·57 m)	4 ft 8½ in. (1·43 m)	34 ft (10·36 m)	6 in. (15·24 cm)	18¾ cwt (888 kg)
Cortina 1300, 1500 and GT from October 1966 to October 1967	14 ft 0 in. (4·27 m)	5 ft 5 in. (1·65 m)	4 ft 8½ in. (1·43 m)	30 ft (9·14 m)	6¼ in. (15·86 cm)	17–17½ cwt (864–890 kg)
Cortina 1300, 1600 and GT from October 1967	14 ft 0 in. (4·27 m)	5 ft 5 in. (1·65 m)	4 ft 6½ in. (1·39 m)	30 ft (9·14 m)	5¼ in. (13·1 cm)	17¼–17¾ cwt (870–904 kg)
Cortina Estate up to February 1967	14 ft 1½ in. (4·31 m)	5 ft 3 in. (1·6 m)	4 ft 8½ in. (1·43 m)	33 ft (10·06 m)	6½ in. (16·51 cm)	17 cwt (864 kg)
Cortina Estate from February 1967	14 ft 1¼ in. (4·30 m)	5 ft 4¾ in. (1·64 m)	4 ft 6½ in. (1·39 m)	30 ft (9·14 m)	5¼ in. (13·1 cm)	18½–19½ cwt (941–966 kg)
Classic	14 ft 3 in. (4·34 m)	5 ft 5 in. (1·65 m)	4 ft 6½ in. (1·39 m)	34 ft (10·36 m)	6½ in. (16·51 cm)	18½–18¾ cwt (941–959 kg)
Corsair 1500 and 1500 GT	14 ft 8½ in. (4·49 m)	5 ft 3½ in. (1·61 m)	4 ft 9½ in. (1·52 m)	36½ ft (11·13 m)	6½ in. (16·51 cm)	17–17¾ cwt (864–904 kg)
Corsair V4, V4 GT, V4 De Luxe, 2000 De Luxe, 2000E	14 ft 8½ in. (4·49 m)	5 ft 3½ in. (1·61 m)	4 ft 9½ in. (1·52 m)	36½ ft (11·13 m)	6½ in. (16·51 cm)	19–20 cwt (966–1017 kg)
Corsair Estate	14 ft 8½ in. (4·49 m)	5 ft 3½ in. (1·61 m)	4 ft 9½ in. (1·52 m)	36½ ft (11·13 m)	6½ in. (16·51 cm)	20½ cwt (1042 kg)

* Approximate figures are given, as the weight will depend on the type of body (2-door, 4-door), equipment fitted, amount of fuel carried and so on.

Fig. 1. The Cortina Super

Fig. 2. The Classic

2 Maintenance in the home garage

SERVICING your car at home pays dividends in more ways than one. For example, if the work is done by a garage, labour charges will form the major part of the bill. This alone is an incentive to the practical owner to tackle as much of the work as possible. Although it may be necessary to purchase some of the basic tools and equipment described later in this chapter, the moderate outlay will quickly be recovered, and—an equally important factor—one has the satisfaction of learning a good deal about one's car and knowing that the work has been done conscientiously, that no greasing points or adjustments have been overlooked or scamped and also that any signs of impending trouble have been detected in good time.

A Practical Home-servicing Scheme. If you own an early Classic or Cortina, you will find that the instruction book will tell you that a number of parts require lubrication at 1,000-mile intervals. From about October 1963 onwards, however, most of the lubrication points were eliminated by the use of plastic bushes and sealed-for-life bearings. This resulted in the period between services being extended to 5,000 miles and nowadays it is considered that a 6,000-mile interval is sufficient. The gaiters on the sealed-for-life steering ball joints of these later models, however, should be checked regularly. If they fail to do their job of retaining lubricant and excluding grit and water, the joints will wear rapidly. These sealed joints incidentally, can be fitted to earlier cars.

In the chart on page 11, you will see that this extended servicing period has been adopted for all models. Research into servicing methods and problems is constantly going on, and the latest recommendations are incorporated in the scheme adopted in this book.

The mileages or periods quoted, therefore, can be substituted for those given in earlier instruction books. Just one word of warning: the extended greasing period depends on the use of a grease containing molybdenum disulphide or colloidal graphite, as these lubricants have a much longer service life than ordinary greases. They can be obtained from most garages nowadays.

An engine oil change should not be deferred beyond the 6,000-mile limit; it may, in fact, be advisable to change the oil more frequently when the car is operating under adverse conditions, as described on page 18.

The routine checks that cannot be tied down to a strict schedule should not be forgotten; i.e. the levels of the engine oil, radiator water and battery electrolyte, and the tyre pressures, all of which should be checked at frequent intervals—at least weekly, and always before starting out on a long run.

Lubrication Chart. The lubrication chart (Fig. 3) applies in general terms to all models but a wall-chart for a particular car is, of course, invaluable, as it enables the various lubrication and servicing parts to be quickly identified and checked-off as work progresses. Fortunately, it is possible to obtain, free of charge, large-scale charts for the garage wall from the Castrol Chart Library, Castrol House, Marylebone Road, London, N.W.1. Just drop them a postcard, mentioning this book and the year and model of your car.

Turning the Engine when Making Adjustments. The fact that modern engines are not provided with starting handles makes it difficult to rotate the crankshaft while setting the valve clearances, adjusting the gap between the contact-breaker points or checking the ignition timing.

The most usual way of overcoming the difficulty is to remove the sparking plugs (to relieve the compression in the cylinders so that the engine will turn freely), engage top gear and then push the car backwards or forward to rotate the engine. This dodge will not work, however, if the car is fitted with an automatic transmission, as there is no positive drive between the crankshaft and the gearbox unless the engine is running.

It is sometimes possible to turn the engine by pulling on the fan blades (taking great care not to bend them), while some owners resort to operating the starting motor for a second or so at a time in the hope of obtaining the correct setting on a hit-and-miss principle. When the solenoid switch in the engine compartment has a rubber-covered button which can be pressed to operate the starter without using the ignition switch, it is in fact usually possible to obtain a reasonably accurate setting if one exercises sufficient patience.

The real answer to the problem, however, is to invest in an ingenious device known as the Junior Autopoints Unit, which is obtainable from Eldred Motors and Electronics Ltd., 855 Holderness Road, Hull, E. Yorks. When this is connected to the battery and starter solenoid switch, the engine can be inched round at the slowest possible speed, making precise adjustment an easy matter.

The device is not cheap, but if you intend to carry out home maintenance as a regular rule, it will soon repay its cost, as it can also be used to set the basic ignition timing, check the actual firing point of the engine, check the condition of the starter ring gear and for other purposes which are described in the instruction leaflet which accompanies the unit.

HOME-SERVICING SCHEME

DAILY
OR EVERY 200 MILES WHEN ON A LONG RUN

Engine Oil Level: Check and top-up if necessary (Chapter 3).
Radiator Header Tank: Check water level (Chapter 4).
Tyre Pressures: Check *when cold*—if checked during run, make allowance for higher pressures. Watch for signs of uneven wear (Chapter 9).

WEEKLY

Battery: Check level of liquid in cells (Chapter 4).

20-POINT CHECK EVERY 6,000 MILES
OR TWICE YEARLY, WHICHEVER OCCURS FIRST

1. **Grease Gun Lubrication:** Lubricate steering joints, pivots and propeller shaft universal joints if nipples are fitted (Chapter 3).
2. **Steering Column Gearchange Mechanism:** Apply oil to joints in linkage.
3. **Handbrake Mechanism:** Relay at rear axle, apply grease. Primary cable engine oil or spray with penetrating oil.
4. **Rear Springs:** Lubricate with engine oil. Check tightness of U-bolts.
5. **Rear Axle:** Check oil level (Chapter 3).
6. **Gearbox:** Check oil level (Chapter 3).
7. **Steering Gearbox:** Check oil level (Chapter 3).
8. **Oilcan Attentions:** Lubricate carburettor controls, door and luggage compartment locks and hinges, rear generator bearing with thin oil.
9. **Engine Lubrication:** Change engine oil and fit new oil filter element. Clean filter in oil filler cap and crankcase emission valve on cross-flow Cortina and V4 engines (Chapter 3).
10. **Ignition Contract-breaker:** Lubricate. Clean and adjust points. Check ignition timing setting (Chapters 3 and 7).
11. **Sparking Plugs:** Clean and adjust. Renew at every second service (Chapter 7).
12. **Fuel Pump:** Clean filter and sediment bowl. Check pipe joints for leaks (Chapter 4).
13. **Carburettor Air Cleaner:** Clean or renew filter element (Chapter 4).
14. **Valve Clearances:** Check and adjust if necessary (Chapter 4).
15. **Carburettor:** Adjust slow-running if necessary (Chapter 4).
16. **Fan Belt:** Check tension and adjust if necessary (Chapter 4).
17. **Brake and Clutch Fluid Reservoirs:** Check fluid levels and top-up if necessary (Chapter 4).
18. **Front Brakes:** Check wear on pads. Look for any signs of brake fluid leakage (Chapter 10).
19. **Rear Brakes:** Remove drums and check linings for wear. Look for any signs of brake fluid or oil leakage. Adjust brakes (Chapter 10).
20. **Clutch:** Check free movement and adjust if necessary (Chapter 4).

FIVE ADDITIONAL JOBS EVERY 18,000 MILES
OR ONCE YEARLY, WHICHEVER COMES FIRST

21. **Front Wheel Bearings:** Repack with grease and adjust (Chapter 3).
22. **Shock Absorbers:** Top-up with correct fluid (Chapter 4).
23. **Steering and Front Suspension:** Have front wheel alignment and steering geometry checked by a Ford dealer (Chapter 9).
24. **Speedometer Driving Cable:** Lubricate.
25. **Cooling System:** Descale and flush out thoroughly Chapter 4).

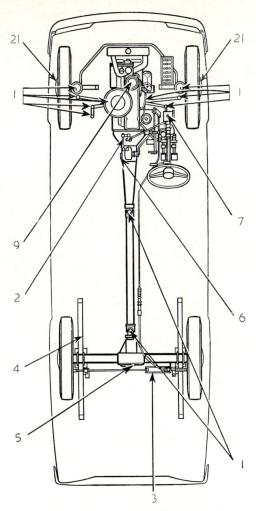

Fig. 3. Lubrication chart

This is generally applicable to all models, but on cars produced from approximately October 1953 onwards the steering linkage and propellor shaft do not require lubrication. The numbers refer to the items in the maintenance schedule opposite

3 Lubrication

IF you are a keen do-it-yourself type, you will not allow the prospect of a certain amount of dirt and discomfort to deter you from getting under the car, say twice a year, to carry out a thorough inspection and lubrication. If, however, you have no facilities for working under the car or if your inclination runs rather to adjustments and profitable tinkering, you may well decide to leave lubrication to the nearest Ford dealer, and you can turn straight away to the more rewarding and interesting work described in other chapters.

Many readers will, however, derive an equal amount of satisfaction from carrying out their own lubrication, perhaps devoting one Saturday morning to the greasing jobs that fall due and leaving the adjustments to be tackled on the following Saturday.

The jobs described in this chapter are those which call for special mention. The other points listed in the maintenance schedule on page 10 should, of course, receive attention. For convenience the work will be grouped under the mileage periods recommended in the schedule. As explained in Chapter II, however, the service periods can be modified to some extent to suit the convenience of the owner.

But first (mainly for the benefit of the novice) we must deal with the very important routine check on the level of the oil in the engine sump.

Checking the Engine Oil Level. The level should be checked at frequent intervals and fresh oil added (if required) to bring the level up to the "Full" mark on the dipstick. Never let the oil fall below the "Danger" mark, but overfilling the sump will simply result in the surplus oil being burnt, which is not only wasteful but will cause unnecessary carbon formation in the cylinders and on the pistons and, if your engine is worn, may result in the sparking plugs becoming oiled up.

Always withdraw and wipe the dipstick, reinsert it and push it fully home, before again withdrawing it to take the actual reading. The car should be standing on level ground and a short time should always be allowed for the oil to drain back into the crankcase: otherwise a misleading reading may be obtained.

If the engine is in good condition, topping-up should be needed only every 200 or 300 miles or at even longer periods when the engine is new; a worn engine, however, will need more frequent checks. Remember too, that the oil consumption will rise in hot weather and will increase quite substantially when long, fast runs are undertaken, compared with the figure that one becomes accustomed to when shorter runs at modest speeds are the order of the day. Tests have shown that the oil does not attain its maximum temperature until the car has been running for approximately one hour.

Choosing the Right Oil. Modern engine oils contain special additives which reduce corrosion of the cylinder walls, prevent the formation of

Fig. 4. The oil level dipstick

sludge and gum and leave the engine in a very clean condition. Multi-grade oils have the added advantage of remaining relatively "thin" even at freezing temperature, thus reducing oil drag during starting and ensuring instant lubrication of the cylinder walls.

It can safely be said that oils marketed by any reputable oil company can be used: for example Castrol, Mobil, Esso, Duckham's, Shell, B.P., Filtrate and Sternol. Oils are identified in most cases, by figures that indicate their thickness or viscosity—for example, an SAE 10w–40 oil is "thinner" than an SAE 20w–50 grade. A range of suitable oils for the engine, and also for the gearbox, rear axle, steering gear and chassis lubrication points, is given in Chapter 1.

When an engine is badly worn, it is an advantage to use the next heavier grade of oil if the oil consumption is on the high side when the normal grade is used—but remember that heavy oil, like aspirin, may relieve the symptoms but does not cure the complaint!

The method of changing the engine oil is described on page 18.

Oil Pressure Gauge Readings. The oil pressure gauge fitted to some models provides the knowledgeable driver with a good deal of useful information. The maximum pressure registered is determined by the setting of the oil-pressure relief valve in the oil pump, which allows some

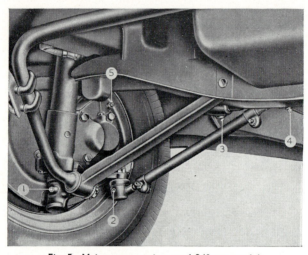

Fig. 5. Maintenance points on 1,340 c.c. models

1. *Track rod control arm lubricator*
2, 4. *Track rod lubricators*

3. *Drop arm lubricator*
5. *Brake bleed nipple—not a lubricator*

of the oil to return to the sump whenever an excessive pressure is likely to be generated in the system—for example, immediately after a cold start, when the viscosity of the oil is relatively high and there is considerable resistance to its passage through the oilways of the engine. The normal oil pressure, at ordinary running speeds, with the engine at its normal temperature and with the oil nicely warmed up after five or ten miles of brisk driving, should be about 35–40 lb per sq in. A much lower pressure —say 5–7 lb per sq in.—will be registered when the engine is idling.

If the pressure is unduly low under normal running conditions, it is as well to seek expert advice as soon as possible. Likely causes, roughly in order of probability, are: insufficient oil in the sump, resulting in the reduced amount of oil becoming overheated and abnormally "thin"; the use of the wrong grade of oil; a sticking pressure relief valve, or a particle of carbon or grit on the seating of the valve; or general wear on the crankshaft and connecting rod bearings.

THE 6,000-MILE SERVICE

The most suitable lubricant to use in the grease gun is one of the modern multipurpose lithium-based greases, treated with molybdenum disulphide. This grease should also be used for packing the front wheel hubs.

Fig. 6. Propeller shaft universal joint

On 1,340 c.c. cars the lubricator requires attention at 6,000-mile intervals. The tightness of the flange nuts should be checked occasionally on all models as looseness will lead to rapid wear

Wipe each lubrication nipple before applying the gun, to avoid any risk of grit being forced through the nipple into the bearing. If the nipple is dented or otherwise damaged it is a simple matter to unscrew it and fit a replacement, which can be obtained from a Ford dealer. In an emergency, however, it is possible to obtain a satisfactory seal, even on a damaged nipple, if a piece of light cloth is placed between the nipple and the end of the grease gun.

Many owners do not realize that every lubrication nipple contains a small spring-loaded ball valve which prevents the grease from escaping from the bearing. If a "worm" of grease exudes from the nipple when the grease gun is removed this valve is not functioning correctly and it is advisable to renew the nipple as soon as possible.

When greasing each steering swivel, jack up that side of the car until the front wheel is clear of the ground. This will allow grease to reach the thrust faces of the bearings that carry the weight.

Gearbox and Rear Axle Lubrication. The rear axle gears require a special "hypoid" or "extreme pressure" gear oil; that used in the rear axle is one grade heavier (*see* Chapter 1). In line with modern practice, the rear axles and gearboxes do not need periodical draining and refilling

Fig. 7. Rear axle casing

1. *Filler and level plug.* 2. *Drain plug (when fitted). It is not necessary to change the oil in normal service.* 3. *Axle breather. Occasionally check that this has not become clogged with mud or sludge; otherwise oil may leak past the axle oil seals*

in service; the gearbox need be drained only after the first 5,000 miles. Subsequently, it is sufficient to top up the axle and gearbox at 5,000-mile intervals.

The combined filler and level plugs are accessible from underneath the car. Clean away all road dirt before unscrewing them, to prevent grit falling into the rear axle. If the oil level is found to be below the level of the filler hole, inject oil until it overflows and then wait until the flow stops before replacing the filler plug.

As the combined filler and level plug is on the back of the rear-axle casing it is rather an awkward job to inject oil unless a piece of rubber tubing is fitted to the spout of a forced-feed oilcan. Alternatively, one of the inexpensive polythene oilcans obtainable from multiple stores, from which the oil is expelled by pressure on the sides of the container, will serve admirably.

Checking Oil Level in Automatic Transmission. When the Borg Warner automatic transmission is fitted, the oil level should be checked during the 6,000-mile service. Just in front of the engine bulkhead, in the engine compartment, there is a filler tube fitted with a breather and dipstick. The oil level should never be checked after the car has been standing for any

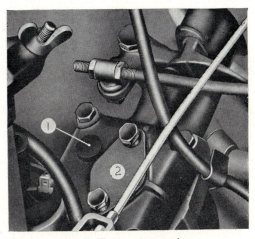

Fig. 8. The steering gearbox

1. Oil filler plug. 2. Steering gearbox cover. Do not disturb this unnecessarily

appreciable time; instead, check it after a run of about five miles, so that the transmission will have reached its normal running temperature. Select the "Park" position and allow the engine to idle for two or three minutes. While it is still ticking over, remove the dipstick, wipe it with a piece of clean paper or a non-fluffy rag, reinsert it and withdraw it immediately.

The difference between the high and low marks on the dipstick represents one imperial pint. Keep the oil level near the top mark but do not overfill the transmission. It is not necessary to drain the oil periodically but it is essential to use only an automatic transmission oil of the type specified on page 1.

Steering Gearbox Lubrication. The steering gearbox has a filler plug on its upper face which must be removed to allow the oil level to be inspected and topped-up if necessary. It is best to make this check with the front wheels turned to full left lock, in the case of right-hand drive cars and full right lock on left-hand drive models.

Miscellaneous Oilcan Attentions. A few drops of thin oil or engine oil should be applied to the following points: the brake and clutch pedal bushes, the carburettor controls; and on cars fitted with steering-column gear-change mechanism, the various pivots and joints in the mechanism. When a floor-mounted lever is fitted, it is advisable to remove the carpet, take off the cover and lubricate the ball joint at the base of the lever.

Items such as door hinges, the bonnet lock and operating mechanism and the boot lid hinges and lock should not be overlooked. Wherever there is any likelihood of oil coming into contact with passengers' clothes, the surplus should be wiped away immediately. To avoid this risk the door lock tongues and catches can be lubricated by rubbing them with an ordinary wax candle.

Dynamo Lubrication. The dynamo requires only two drops of engine oil in the lubrication hole provided in the bearing plate at the opposite end to the driving pulley. The bearing at the pulley end is self-lubricating.

Changing the Engine Oil. The engine oil becomes contaminated with carbon and other products of combustion, including condensed water and fuel, and must, therefore, be drained out at least at 6,000-mile intervals, as explained in Chapter 2, when the filter element should also be renewed. If the engine is worn, the degree of gas leakage past the piston rings may make it advisable to change the oil more frequently; for example, it is sometimes recommended that a change at 3,000 miles shows some economy in the long run, since, by maintaining the quality of the oil, the overall consumption is reduced. Also, more frequent changes are advisable when most of the driving is done in cold weather, particularly when frequent starts are made from cold and when the engine is allowed to idle for long periods. At the other extreme, in hot, dusty conditions the oil will deteriorate more quickly than in temperate climates. Under really adverse conditions it may even be advisable to change the oil as frequently as every 1,000 miles. If in doubt, consult your local Ford dealer.

The oil should be drained when the car has just come in from a run; being hot, it will be more fluid and will be holding in suspension the impurities.

If a modern premium oil is used, it should not be necessary to flush out the sump with flushing oil, as was often recommended with older types of car. As the sump will contain from four to seven pints of oil, depending on the model, a sufficiently large drain pan should be provided. An old kitchen washing-up bowl will serve admirably. Sufficient time should be allowed for the oil to drain completely before the drain plug is replaced.

The sump should then be refilled until the level is up to the "Full" mark on the dipstick.

Renewing the Oil Filter Element. Clean the exterior of the oil filter casing and the upper casting. The filter bolt can then be slackened. Then,

Fig. 9. Engine oil filter fitted on all engines except the V4 range

1. *Retaining bolt*   3. *Sealing ring*
2. *Oil pressure warning light switch*   4. *Filter body*

working from below, the bolt can be unscrewed, the casing withdrawn and the filter cartridge lifted out.

The new element will be supplied complete with new sealing washers. The filter bowl should be thoroughly cleaned before the new element is inserted and the washers positioned as indicated in the instructions packed with the element. Remove the old rubber sealing ring from the groove in the casting and press the new ring carefully into place, beginning at four diametrically opposite points. If you start at one point and work the gasket around the groove, it will stretch and form a kink that will cause an oil leak.

On V4 engines the complete filter—a combined casing and element—must be unscrewed from the left-hand side of the engine and a replacement fitted. If the filter is too tight to be unscrewed by hand, use a strap-tool or tap it round with a drift to free it.

As soon as the engine is running, examine the filter for leakage. A very pronounced leak will occur if the bowl is slightly displaced and does not seat squarely on the sealing ring.

Lubricating the Distributor. Remove the moulded cap from the distributor by springing aside the two retaining clips. The rotor should then be pulled or gently levered off the end of the central shaft, exposing a screw within a recess in the shaft to which a few drops of engine oil should be applied. It is not necessary to remove the screw; a clearance exists between it and the inner face of the spindle through which oil can reach the spindle bearing.

While the rotor is off, lightly smear the faces of the cam with a very small amount of grease. Over-lubrication should be avoided owing to the risk of grease being thrown on to the contact points, where it will become carbonized and cause misfiring. A few drops of light engine oil should also be squirted through the hole in the contact-breaker base-plate through which the distributor spindle passes and just a spot of oil should be placed on the pivot pin on which the moving contact arm swivels. Again over-generous lubrication can do more harm than good.

Do not forget to replace the rotor and make sure that the driving lug on its underside engages correctly with the slot in the spindle. Push it home as far as possible.

THE 18,000-MILE SERVICE

Front Hub Lubrication. An important job which is necessary at the 18,000-mile period is the lubrication of the front wheel hubs. Strictly speaking, the hub bearings should be dismantled so that the races may be cleaned and examined for wear, before being relubricated with fresh grease. The need for careful adjustment of the end-float in the taper roller bearings on reassembly, however, suggests that this job is best left to a Ford dealer, but when necessary the work should be tackled as described below.

Jack up the car, remove the wheel and carefully lever the dust cap from the end of the hub.

From this point the procedure will depend on whether the brakes are of the drum or the disc type.

When dealing with drum brakes, slacken off the two square-headed adjusters which protrude from the brake backplate, by turning them anticlockwise. Remove the split pin from the slotted adjusting nut, unscrew the nut and slide off the thrust washer and the outer taper roller bearing. The hub and drum assembly can now be pulled off the stub axle.

Check the condition of the brake linings and operating cylinders as detailed on pages 113–14. The hub bearings can then be cleaned and lubricated, as described below.

When disc brakes are fitted to the front wheels, it will be necessary to remove the brake callipers before the hubs can be drawn off.

When the retaining pin clips and the two retaining pins that locate the brake pads in the calliper have been removed, mark the brake pads (spots of paint will do) to indicate their positions, as they must be refitted in the same locations. The pads may now be removed, with their shims.

From the suspension unit side of the calliper, tap back the calliper mounting bolt locking tabs, that form part of a small splash shield, and unscrew the bolts.

The calliper can now be moved aside and supported on a box to avoid stressing the fluid pipe.

Next the hub is withdrawn after extracting the spindle split pin, unscrewing the bearing adjusting nut and taking off the thrust washer and outer bearing.

Wash these components, together with the inner bearing, in clean paraffin and repack both bearings with a good quality lithium-base molybdenum disulphide grease, working the grease carefully into the rollers and cages.

The hub itself should not be packed completely full. An appreciable air space should be left. If the inner bearing has been removed, refit it and then replace the hub and outer bearing on the spindle followed by the thrust washer and castellated nut.

Strictly speaking a torque wrench should be used to tighten the bearing adjusting nut to between 14 and 17 lb-ft whilst rotating the disc. The nut should then be slackened back by not less than two and one-half, and not more than three, castellations. Fit a new split pin, clean and replace the dust cap on the hub.

You may be able to borrow or hire a torque wrench from a garage but if not, tighten the bearing adjusting nut whilst rotating the disc until a heavy drag can just be felt. Then turn back the nut one split-pin location at a time until the hub is perfectly free, with just perceptible end-float.

Refit the calliper, and a *new* small splash shield, to the mounting bracket, tightening the two mounting bolts to a torque of 40 to 45 lb-ft. Bend up the locking tabs on the splash shield to secure the bolts.

Refit the brake pads and shims in the positions from which they were removed, with the arrows on the shims pointing in the forward direction of rotation of the hub and disc. Replace the retaining pins and clips.

4 Routine servicing and adjustments

In this chapter it is proposed to describe the jobs which you can tackle confidently, even if you are a novice, with the tools likely to be found in the average home garage. It will thus be possible to leave the more ambitious work to later chapters, in which the specialized aspects can be dealt with in greater detail for the benefit of more experienced owners. "Vital statistics"—clearances, pressures, oil and water capacities and so on—are summarized in Chapter 1.

We can begin with the checks which should be carried out at least weekly, and possibly daily if a large mileage is being covered—for example, during the course of a holiday tour it is advisable to check the water level in the radiator and to test the tyre pressure at the beginning of each day's run.

Topping-up the Radiator. Although the water level in the radiator header tank should be checked regularly and frequently, topping-up should seldom be necessary if the cooling system is free from leaks. The filler cap is fitted with a spring-loaded valve that maintains a modest pressure in the system when the engine is hot, thus raising the boiling point and also preventing loss of water.

If the engine is at its normal running temperature, wrap the cap in a cloth before removing it. Turn it progressively to allow the pressure to escape, before finally lifting it off, because if the engine is overheated, violent boiling can start when the pressure is released.

The level should be about one inch below the base of the filler neck. Don't top-up the radiator when the engine is cold; this will only lead to unnecessary loss of water (and relatively expensive anti-freeze solution, when this is in use), as the water in the system will expand when the engine warms up, the valve will open and the excess will escape through the overflow pipe.

A possible cause of water leakage is chafing of the heater hose against the rocker cover. This can be cured by shortening the hose by $\frac{1}{2}$ in.—a modification which was introduced early in 1964.

Anti-freezing Solutions. When anti-freeze is used it is not advisable to top-up with pure water. Although the anti-freeze ingredient in the cooling water does not evaporate, the need for fairly frequent topping-up indicates that the coolant must be escaping through a leak at some point and the addition of water will weaken the mixture—possibly to a dangerous extent. When the leak has been discovered and cured, anti-freeze solution of the recommended strength must be used to restore the correct level and thus prevent the remaining solution being diluted.

Anti-freeze should always be used when there is any risk of the temperature falling below freezing point but it is advisable first to descale and flush-out the cooling system as described on page 36. It is unwise to rely on the doubtful precaution of draining the system overnight. If an interior heater is fitted, in fact, it is essential to use anti-freeze, as the

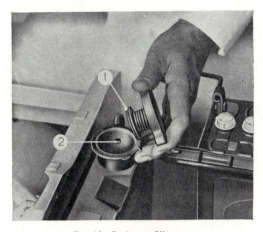

Fig. 10. Radiator filler cap

1. *Check that the pressure relief valve is in good condition.* 2. *Make sure that the overflow hole and pipe are not clogged*

heater element cannot be drained completely by opening the radiator and cylinder-block drain taps and frost may damage it.

Any of the well-known brands of anti-freeze will be quite satisfactory. The correct amount to use will be stated on the container or in a leaflet or chart obtainable from the supplier.

Many anti-freeze manufacturers claim that a given proportion (usually 20 per cent, representing about $2\frac{1}{2}$ pints of anti-freeze in the cooling systems of these cars) will protect against 35°F of frost. This statement should, however, be treated with reserve. It is true that there will be no risk of a cracked cylinder block or a damaged radiator, but the solution will have formed ice crystals and its "mushy" condition will prevent adequate flow through the system. When the thermometer drops to these Arctic levels the engine must be allowed to idle for at least five minutes after being started from cold, preferably with the radiator covered, to allow the system to warm up. In order to obtain complete protection at very low temperatures—in the neighbourhood of 0°F or about −18°C— a mixture consisting of about equal volumes of anti-freeze and water is required. This is a point that doctors and others who may wish to drive away from cold without delay should bear in mind.

The anti-freeze can be left in the system during the summer months, but it is better to drain it off in the spring, since the anti-corrosion inhibitors which are incorporated in the ethylene–glycol mixture may tend to lose their effectiveness over a prolonged period of use—and untreated glycol is very corrosive. In any case the system will probably benefit from flushing out and refilling with new anti-freeze.

Curing Leaks. Proprietary chemical anti-leak compounds are usually quite effective in curing small leakages, but even a first-class compound will not be effective if it builds-up on top of deposits of scale or rust; the most satisfactory course, therefore, is thoroughly to flush-out and descale the system, as described on page 36, before using one of these compounds.

Tyre Pressures are Vital. It is essential to use an accurate pressure gauge when checking the tyre pressures (which are listed in Chapter 1). Protect the gauge from knocks and grit when it is not in use. Garage airline gauges cannot always be relied on. In any case, the pressures should be taken when the tyres are cold and even a short run is sufficient to warm them up and cause an appreciable rise in pressure.

Whenever the pressures have been checked, make sure that the valve caps have been replaced and tightened firmly. These are intended to prevent leakage and at the same time exclude mud, grit and ice from the relatively vulnerable inner seals. If a cap should be lost, a replacement should be fitted as soon as possible.

If the tyres are fitted with inner tubes, pressure will be lost at the rate of from 1 to 3 lb per week, owing to a process known as "diffusion." Oxygen from the air in the tyre is absorbed by the rubber and a corresponding amount of oxygen is given off from the outer surface of the tube. It is necessary, therefore, to restore this slight loss of pressure even when the tubes are in first-class condition. Synthetic rubber tubes and tubeless tyres do not suffer so much from this disadvantage but it is still advisable to check the pressures regularly, as slight leakage usually occurs.

Topping-up the Battery Cells. On modern cars on which the battery is carried in the engine compartment, the liquid in the cells (termed the electrolyte) tends to evaporate rather quickly, especially in hot weather. The level in each cell should, therefore, be checked at weekly intervals. Don't allow it to fall below the tops of the separators between the plates, or the perforated separator guard, as the case may be.

Distilled water should be added if necessary until the correct level is reached in each cell. Never use tapwater or rainwater, which usually contain impurities that will shorten the life of the battery. A "free" source of distilled water is that which condenses in the drip tray of a refrigerator when the freezing coils are defrosted—but this does *not* apply to water obtained by melting ice cubes!

Never use a naked flame when inspecting the level of the fluid in the cells, as an explosive mixture of hydrogen and oxygen may be present.

It is best to add water just before the cells are to be charged. In cold weather this will allow the acid and water to mix thoroughly and will thus avoid any risk of the water freezing and damaging the plates and battery case. Incidentally, it is always risky to leave a battery in a discharged state during very cold weather. If it does freeze, the only cure will be a new battery! A trickle-charger is a good investment, as explained in Chapter 8.

It should not be necessary to add acid to the cells unless some of the electrolyte has been spilt, in which case a Ford dealer should be consulted. If acid is added in order to raise the specific gravity of the electrolyte, the plates may be damaged.

The need for excessive topping-up of all the cells usually suggests an unduly high generator charging rate. Have the regulator setting checked by a *qualified* electrician. If one cell regularly requires more water than the others, a leak in that cell must be suspected.

THE 6,000-MILE SERVICE

Servicing the Ignition System. A smoothly-running engine, even and reliable idling, easy starting, and good power output combined with economical petrol consumption, all depend to a large extent on the sparking plugs and the ignition distributor. The method of cleaning the plugs and setting the gaps is dealt with in detail in Chapter 7, where details are also given of the attention to the ignition contact-breaker points, which falls due at this mileage.

Servicing Carburettor Air Cleaner. The air filter fitted to the carburettor air intake may be one of three types: oil-bath, dry-gauze, or paper-element.

A serious fault which has cropped up on some Cortinas is breakage of the threaded part of the air-cleaner retaining bolt. The broken piece can work out of the threads in the carburettor stirrup, fall into the carburettor intake and be drawn into a combustion chamber past an inlet valve, seriously damaging the piston and cylinder head. To prevent the trouble, the manufacturers introduced a thicker bolt and a modified stirrup, which should be fitted as replacements.

The mileage at which an oil-bath air cleaner needs attention will depend, of course, on the conditions under which the car is driven. Under dusty conditions it will need more frequent attention, but 5,000 miles is normal.

Remove the filter, keeping it upright, unscrew the wing nut at the top of the cleaner and lift the cover and filter unit from the body. Empty the oil and clean out any accumulation of sludge. The filter should be washed in petrol and the air cleaner body filled with fresh engine oil up to the level of the arrow.

If a dry-gauze type air cleaner is fitted, remove the top cover, wash the

Fig. 11. Pleated paper air cleaner (*left*) and alternative gauze type (*right*)

element in petrol, allow it to dry and then dip it in engine oil. Shake off the surplus oil before refitting the element.

If your car has a paper-element filter the element should be replaced after 18,000 miles. No intermediate servicing should normally be necessary but in extremely dusty areas it could be beneficial to remove the paper element every 6,000 miles, shake it clean or carefully brush off the dust and refit it. Before fitting a new element, remove the sealing ring from the top cover and the one beneath the element in the cleaner body and fit new rings.

Fuel Pump Filter. The A.C. mechanically-operated petrol pump needs little attention, other than to keep the filter free from dirt and sediment. At 6,000-mile intervals, remove the domed filter cover or the glass bowl,

swill the gauze filter in petrol and clean out any sediment that has accumulated in the filter chamber.

The tightness of the nut securing the filter cover or bowl should be
checked from time to time. An air leak at the flange—which will also
occur if the cork sealing ring is cracked or chipped—is one of the most

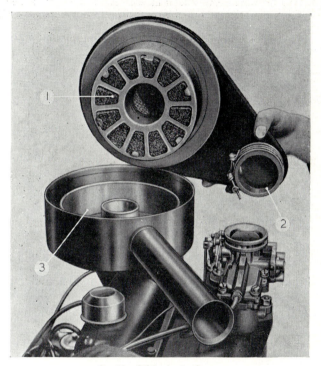

Fig. 12. Oil bath air cleaner
1. *Filter element.* 2. *Connexion to carburettor.* 3. *Oil bath*

common causes of pump failure. The fuel pipe unions should also be
checked over.

Valve Clearance Adjustment. To keep your engine in good tune, check
the valve clearances at 5,000-mile intervals and if necessary reset them to
the figures given in Chapter 1. This is particularly important on overhead-
valve engines. If there is noticeable tapping or clicking from the valve

2

cover on top of the engine, however, or if the car seems to lack power
or liveliness, the tappet clearances should be checked without waiting
for the routine service to fall due.

The term tappet clearance or valve clearance refers to the gap that
should be maintained between the tip of the rocker (which depresses the
valve) and the valve stem itself. If the clearance is too small, there is a
risk of the valve being held open because the parts expand as the engine

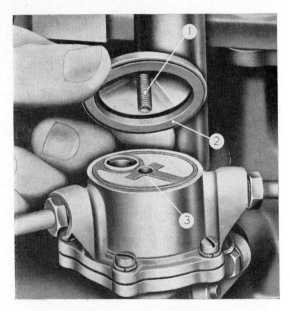

Fig. 13. Earlier type of petrol pump
1. *Cover retaining bolt.* 2. *Sealing ring.* 3. *Filter gauze*

warms up. This will cause loss of power and burnt valve seatings. If the
clearances are too great, on the other hand, the valve gear will be noisy
and the valves will open too late and close too early, seriously reducing
both power and maximum speed.

The valve gear is exposed when the valve cover has been removed, as
shown in Fig. 15. To check the clearances, turn the engine until a valve
has just fully closed and then give the engine a further half-turn to ensure
that the cam is free of the tappet. The easiest way to turn the engine is
to remove all the sparking plugs and to pull on the fan belt. As the plugs

should be removed for inspection and the gaps reset at this mileage, one thus kills two birds with one stone!

Insert a feeler blade between the toe of the rocker and the tip of the valve stem. If the gap is not correct, on an in-line engine loosen the lock-nut and turn the adjusting screw with a screwdriver until the correct

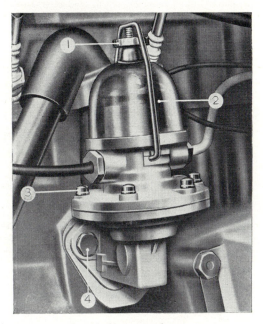

Fig. 14. Later petrol pump

The filter bowl 2 is retained by the thumb nut 1. Occasionally check the tightness of the screws 3. If they are loose, an air leak can put the pump out of action. Loose bolts 4 will cause an oil leak at the mounting flange

clearance is obtained. Hold it in this position while tightening the lock-nut. Apply a firm pressure to the screwdriver while checking the clearance in order to displace all but a thin film of oil from the cupped ends of the tappet and push-rod. A false reading may otherwise be obtained.

After tightening the lock-nut, re-check the clearance, as this will usually be found to change the adjustment slightly. One or two attempts may be necessary before an accurate clearance is obtained.

On V4 engines, the method of adjustment is different. Each rocker arm is individually mounted on a stud which is pressed into the cylinder head and pivots against a spherical face on the underside of a self-locking nut. Screwing the nut downwards will therefore move the rocker closer to the valve and push-rod, reducing the clearance, whereas screwing it upwards will increase the clearance.

It is advisable to use two feeler gauges to check the adjustment—one which is one-thousandth of an inch (0·001 in.) too large and which should

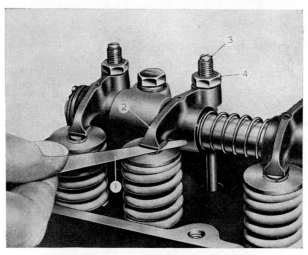

Fig. 15. Checking the tappet clearances

A feeler gauge 1 is used to measure the clearance between the rocker 2 and the tip of the valve. On in-line engines the adjusting screw 3 is locked by the nut 4

not enter, and one which is one-thousandth too small, which should enter easily.

Remember that if the cylinder-head bolts are tightened down, the valve clearances will be reduced.

Before replacing the valve rocker cover, inspect the cover gasket. If there is any doubt regarding its condition it should be renewed. Make sure that the cover is seating evenly on the cylinder head and is located correctly before tightening the securing screws evenly.

Carburettor Slow-running Adjustment. When the sparking plugs have been cleaned, the contact-breaker points trued-up and adjusted and the tappet clearances checked, it is usually an advantage to readjust the carburettor idling mixture strength slightly, to obtain a really smooth tick-over and a good pick-up from low speeds. This job is fully described in Chapter 6

Check the Fan Belt Tension. The fan belt, which also drives the generator or dynamo, should be kept free from grease and should be correctly tensioned. There should be a free movement of $\frac{1}{2}$ in. at the centre of the belt between the fan and generator pulleys when it is pushed and pulled. If the belt is too slack, it will slip; on the other hand, if it is too tightly adjusted, excessive wear will occur on the fan and generator bearings.

Fig. 16. Dynamo and fan belt adjustment

1. *Adjusting bolt on slotted strut.* 2. *Pivot bolts, which must also be slackened to allow the dynamo to be moved when adjusting the belt tension*

It is a simple matter to adjust the tension by loosening the two mounting bolts on the generator and the clamping bolt on the strut, allowing the generator to be swung towards or away from the engine. To increase the tension on the belt, pull the generator outwards; do not use any leverage. After the mounting bolts and strut clamping bolt have been tightened, re-check the free movement of the belt.

If the belt squeaks, a little brake fluid—*not* oil—will stop the noise; or dust it with french chalk.

Brake and Clutch Fluid Reservoirs. The clutch and brake fluid reservoirs are mounted on the bulkhead in the engine compartment. Wipe them clean before unscrewing the caps to check the fluid levels. Top-up, if necessary, to within $\frac{1}{2}$ in. of the top of each reservoir, using the specified fluid (Chapter 1). If this is not available, any alternative fluid which conforms to the specification SAE 70R3 may be used.

It should be emphasized that this is, primarily, a precautionary check. If the systems are in good condition, topping-up should be required only at very long intervals. But leaks *can* develop from hydraulic pipelines and screwed unions, or past rubber seals in the operating cylinders; and loss of fluid from the braking system could have disastrous results. Alternatively, if the clutch-operating system is affected, it will be impossible to free the clutch completely, thus virtually immobilizing the car.

If the level of the fluid in either reservoir has fallen appreciably, therefore, have an assistant apply firm pressure to the appropriate pedal while

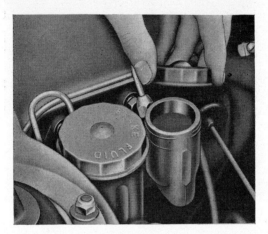

Fig. 17. Brake and clutch fluid reservoirs

you examine the pipelines and operating cylinders for any signs of leakage. If slight leakage has occurred—say, from a slack union—it may not be sufficient simply to tighten the union and top-up the reservoir; air may have entered the system, giving the pedal a characteristically "spongy" feel. The method of bleeding off the air is described in Chapter 10.

Up to about April 1963 the seals in the master cylinders tended to leak very slightly—it was seepage rather than leakage and was not serious—but if the trouble is encountered on an early model it can be cured by fitting the later type of seal. Prior to August in the same year the pivot bolts that link the pedals to the master cylinder push-rods could work loose. In this case a modified bolt is the answer.

A further point: check that the air vent holes in the filler caps of the reservoirs are clear. If they become choked, there is a risk of the brakes dragging or the clutch slipping, depending on which reservoir is affected.

Checking and Adjusting the Brakes. Although any major shortcomings in the braking system will, of course, have shown up during normal running, slight but progressive deterioration in braking efficiency inevitably takes place as the linings wear and the process is so gradual that it usually goes undetected by a driver who becomes familiar with the car and sub-consciously adjusts himself to changes in its running. A critical reassessment of the braking efficiency at 5,000-mile intervals, therefore, is a useful check on this subconscious adjustment of values. As a number of factors

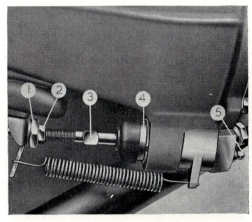

Fig. 18. Clutch adjustment

1. *Adjusting nut*	4. *Clutch operating cylinder*
2. *Lock-nut*	5. *Air bleed valve*
3. *Push-rod*	

affect braking efficiency, testing, adjustments, and the method of removing the brake drums so that the linings can be inspected for wear and the hydraulic cylinders checked for leakage, are dealt with in some detail in Chapter 10.

Changing the Tyres Around. Apart from regular pressure checks, longer life can be obtained from a set of tyres by equalizing, as far as possible, the wear on the individual treads. This calls for changing the wheels around. Fig. 51 (page 111) shows alternative schemes with the choice depending on whether a reliable tyre is fitted to the spare wheel. At the same time examine the treads carefully and prise out any flints or other sharp objects. The tyres are discussed more fully in Chapter IX.

Clutch Adjustment. The friction linings on the driven plate of the clutch wear down and the slight free movement that should exist at the clutch pedal will gradually be taken up. On Cortina 1300 and 1600 and V4 Corsair models there is automatic compensation for this wear but on other cars there is a risk of the clutch beginning to slip under load, causing overheating and rapid deterioration of the linings.

A free movement of about one inch must therefore be maintained at the pedal. This represents a clearance between the end of the adjusting nut and the clutch release arm of $\frac{1}{10}$ in. (*see* Fig. 16).

To obtain the correct clearance, disconnect the release arm retracting spring, slacken the operating rod lock-nut and turn the domed adjusting

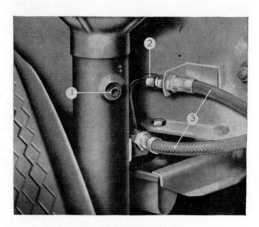

Fig. 19. Front suspension unit

1. *Combined filler and level plug. Check the tightness of the brake pipeline unions 2 and the hoses 3 for fraying or kinking*

nut at the end of the push-rod clockwise to increase the free movement, and anticlockwise to reduce it.

After making the adjustment, make sure that the lock-nut is tightened and the return spring is hooked in place.

If the clutch does not free properly when the adjustment is correct, the trouble must lie at some point within the clutch mechanism and will call for specialist attention.

When clutch judder develops the most likely cause is worn or glazed friction linings, a defective centre-plate or internal release mechanism. If the pedal has a "spongy" action, it will be necessary to bleed air from the hydraulic system of later clutches as described in Chapter 10 when dealing with the brakes. There is a bleed nipple on the clutch-operating cylinder.

Crankcase Fume-Emission Valve. On Cortina cross-flow and on Corsair V4 engines a positive crankcase ventilation system is used. Fumes are drawn into the inlet manifold through a regulating valve which is a push-fit in a grommet in the oil-separator at the rear of the Cortina engine, on the right-hand side, and in the right-hand rocker cover on V4 engines. The valve must be cleaned at 6,000-mile intervals, or whenever the engine oil is changed.

Disconnect the hose and pull the valve out of its grommet in the cover. Dismantle it by removing the circlip and extracting the valve seal, valve and spring, all of which should be washed in petrol. Do not run the engine with the hose disconnected from the valve as the excessive amount of air entering the inlet manifold will provide too weak a mixture.

THE 18,000-MILE SERVICE

Three of the jobs that must be done at this mileage are dealt with in other chapters (*see* the maintenance schedule on page 10). We are left, therefore, with topping-up the shock absorbers if the units have filler plugs and with the seasonal attentions to the cooling system, which are particularly important in maintaining the efficiency of a modern engine.

Front Suspension Units. To inject shock-absorber fluid into each front suspension unit (and into the rear shock absorbers) calls for a "squirt" oilcan with a long spout. *The can must be scrupulously clean*, as any trace of oil will damage the seals in the units. It is better to keep a can specially for this job. Before checking the fluid level in each front suspension unit, make sure that the car is parked on level ground, unladen.

The combined filler and level plug in each suspension unit body, approximately 3 in. below the coil spring lower seat at the front or rear of the unit, should be removed, and shock-absorber fluid added until the level reaches the bottom of the plug hole. Do not add fluid to the suspension units under pressure. Replace and tighten the plug.

Rear Shock Absorbers. On early cars each rear shock absorber has a filler plug at the side of the housing and if necessary shock absorber fluid should be added until the level reaches the filler plug orifice. This attention should not normally be required.

Cooling System Maintenance. Sometimes one encounters a stubborn case of overheating, usually combined with persistent pinking and, often, running-on when the ignition is switched off. These symptoms point to overheated exhaust valves and sparking plugs and a likely cause is corrosion or clogging of the water distribution passages in the cylinder head or in the cylinder block.

If descaling and flushing the cooling system as described below is not effective, it would be as well to consult a Ford dealer; but the best policy is to carry out regularly the preventive maintenance described.

At least once a year, then—preferably twice, in the autumn and in the spring, if an anti-freezing compound is used—the system should be drained, flushed-out and refilled. If the water does not flow freely from the radiator drain tap and from the tap on the side of the engine cylinder block, probe the openings with a piece of wire to dislodge any accumulated sediment—or better still, unscrew and remove the taps. A hose should then be inserted in the filler neck and water allowed to flow through the system until clean water issues from the taps.

Before flushing the system it is an advantage to run the car for a day or two with a proprietary non-corrosive descaling compound added to the cooling water. These compounds will remove any deposits of rust or scale which might be sealing minor leaks. If anti-freezing compound is used without descaling the system, there is a risk that its very "searching" action may find such weak spots, possibly with serious consequences if a leak should develop and continue undetected during the course of a lengthy run.

To prevent any risk of slight leakage or the possibility of anti-freeze seeping past the cylinder-head gasket into the cylinders, where it can cause a gummy mess which will result in serious trouble, the use of an anti-leak compound is well worthwhile. "Bars Leaks" is excellent. It also keeps the system clean, preventing corrosion and the building-up of rust and scale deposits.

If an interior heater is fitted and the cooling system has been drained, make sure that the heater water-control tap is open when refilling the radiator. It is a good plan to slacken the clamp on the upper heater hose, and to loosen the hose in order to dispel any air-lock that may develop in the heater. Do not tighten the clamp until water is flowing from this point and re-check the level in the header tank after the engine has been running for a few minutes.

The Thermostat. The thermostat, which regulates the cooling water temperature and vitally affects engine efficiency, is often overlooked and seldom checked. It consists of a valve operated by a bellows or a wax-filled capsule, fitted at the water outlet from the cylinder head, that prevents circulation of water to the radiator until the normal running temperature is reached.

The valve should be fully open before the water in the cooling system approaches boiling point.

Thermostats, of course, are not infallible and if overheating occurs, or conversely, if the engine is slow to warm-up, it is logical to check this item. Remember, however, that overheating can be caused by a number of other faults, among which deposits of rust and lime scale in the cylinder head and radiator water passages are the most likely. Shortage of oil or water, obstructed air passages in the radiator, over-retarded ignition and severe pinking will also cause the trouble.

The thermostat can be lifted out after the water outlet elbow has been removed. When cold the valve should be tightly closed. If it is open, either the bellows is punctured or the stem is jammed by an accumulation of lime deposits.

If the thermostat appears to be serviceable, test it by immersing it in a pan of water, which is nearly at boiling point. If a suitable thermometer is available, the opening temperature can be checked while moving the thermostat about in the water as it is heated. If the valve has not opened when the water begins to boil, a replacement should be fitted. Before refitting a used thermostat, make sure that the small air-release hole in the valve is not choked; otherwise an air-lock is likely to occur when the cooling system is refilled.

Cortina Bonnet Catch. A final point: as soon as you open the bonnet of an early Cortina you will see a potential source of trouble—the bent-wire safety catch. This can be distorted if it catches on the clothing of anyone who is working under the bonnet and can then be bent double when the bonnet is slammed down. It thus ceases to do its job as a safety catch and may even prevent the main catch engaging properly, allowing the bonnet to fly open when the car is travelling at speed.

A pressed-steel catch is fitted to later models and can be substituted for the wire type. Keep the catch spring and spindle well lubricated to prevent rust, and grease the plunger of the main catch from time to time.

5 Decarbonizing and valve-grinding

SOONER or later, perhaps not until 30,000 miles have been covered or perhaps at an earlier stage if most of your running is of the stop-start variety or your engine is no longer in its first youth and is consuming a moderate amount of oil, it will be necessary to remove the cylinder head in order to decarbonize the piston crowns and combustion chambers and to grind-in the valves.

Strictly speaking, the latter attention is the more important nowadays, especially if an engine is in reasonably good condition, as modern oils and fuels cause only light carbon deposits. An efficient overhead-valve engine as fitted to these models, on the other hand, will quickly lose its liveliness if the valve faces and seatings become pitted or burnt. In view of the importance of periodical attention to the valves, therefore, it would be fairer to term the job a top-overhaul rather than decarbonizing in the older sense of the word.

What are the symptoms that suggest a top-overhaul is due? When the engine begins to lose power, starting becomes more difficult and pinking is evident when it is pulling hard at low speeds, even when premium fuel is in use and the ignition timing has been retarded by, say, one division on the scale of the micrometer control on the ignition distributor (*see* Chapter 7), it is probable that the time has come to put it into dock for a couple of days while the work is carried out. It is a good axiom never to disturb an engine that is running well; but if a top-overhaul is postponed for too long, more harm than good can be done.

Most service stations can check the compression of each cylinder with the aid of a special pressure gauge. If the compression is weak on one or more cylinders the most likely cause is burnt or pitted valve faces. Leakage of gases past the piston rings cannot, of course, be discounted, but this fault will normally be accompanied by excessive oil consumption.

Apart from the compression test, a reliable indication of the general condition of the engine can be obtained by the use of a manifold vacuum gauge of the type that is included, for example, in the Redex Do-it-yourself Tuning Kit, following the detailed instructions for engine testing that are supplied with the particular kit. A practical owner will quickly find such a gauge invaluable, not only for diagnosing such faults as burnt or sticking valves, worn piston rings and defective sparking plugs, but also for carrying out carburettor and ignition timing adjustments.

Can the work be done in the home garage? If you have reasonable ability in handling simple tools, the answer is "Yes." The great advantage of doing the work yourself, of course, is the saving in the cost of valuable man-hours; as the job will take between four and eight hours, depending on how expert you are, the saving will be considerable, when labour at the local garage may cost as much as £2 an hour nowadays.

If you have not tackled the job on a previous car, allow a full week-end for the work. For example if you make a start on Friday evening, you should be able to clean down the engine thoroughly with paraffin or Gunk (which is excellent for dealing with oil and grime), get the cylinder

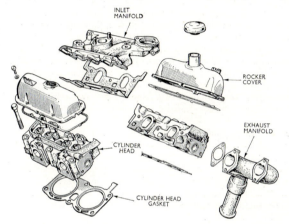

Fig. 20. Cylinder heads, inlet and exhaust manifolds of V4 engines

head off and carry out a thorough inspection. Any replacement items that may be needed, in addition to the normal decarbonizing kit described below, can then be purchased on Saturday morning, when most garages and spares counters are open.

Tools and Spares Required. Before starting work it is necessary to assemble, in addition to the usual tools used for routine maintenance, a valve-spring compressor (it may be possible to hire this from a local garage, as it will not be required again until the engine is next decarbonized), a blunt scraper, a tin of valve-grinding paste containing both fine and coarse grades, a plentiful supply of clean rags, free from fluff, a selection of boxes, tins or jars in which small parts can be deposited, pending reassembly, a wire brush, paraffin and a dish or tray in which to swill the parts.

It is advisable to renew all gaskets. The expense is small and is an insurance against water or gas leakages after the engine has been re-assembled, which would, of course, entail the dismantling and reassembly of the parts. If a defective cylinder-head gasket allows water to leak into the cylinders, serious damage may be done. Again, although no external leakage may be apparent, gas may leak between adjacent cylinders, where the gasket is narrow and is subject to relatively high pressure, causing misfiring and loss of power which may be difficult to diagnose.

A set of new valve springs is a worthwhile investment. If the top-overhaul is carried out properly it can be expected that the car will run for upwards of 20,000 miles before the head is next removed; but "tired" valve springs can undo all the careful work put into the overhaul.

A couple of spare exhaust valves will insure against the possibility of finding, when the head has been removed, that one or two of the valves are too badly pitted to be salvaged by grinding-in. Inlet valves seldom require renewal but for the Cortina cross-flow and the V4 engine it is as well to purchase one of these also. It can then be used as a "slave" to clean up the seatings in the cylinder head, as described on pages 44–6.

When purchasing these parts, ask the dealer whether he can let you have an old piston ring which will fit the bores; this will be useful when decarbonizing the pistons, as described later.

Removing the Cylinder Head. Considering first the in-line engine (the V4 power units are dealt with on pages 41–2), begin by draining the cooling system. Disconnect the battery cables and remove the battery. Disconnect the sparking-plug leads and number each to avoid confusion on reassembly. At this stage it is advisable to remove the sparking plugs, putting them aside for cleaning and resetting of the gaps. Detach the wire from the engine temperature gauge transmitter, on the near side of the engine, behind the fan.

Remove the air cleaner and disconnect the carburettor throttle and choke controls, the petrol pipe and the vacuum pipe to the distributor. The carburettor may now be removed.

Slacken the securing clips and remove the radiator hose and the heater hose at the cylinder head (if fitted).

Disconnect the exhaust pipe at the silencer inlet pipe joint, and remove the exhaust manifold in the case of GT engines. The manifold-securing nuts can now be removed and the manifolds taken off.

Attention should next be turned to the valve rocker shaft assembly. Remove the rocker cover from the top of the cylinder and unscrew the nuts that retain the rocker shaft brackets. The rocker assembly can then be lifted off.

The eight push-rods that operate the rockers should next be withdrawn one at a time, giving each a twist to break the suction of the oil in the hollow tappets. Lay them out in order in a place where they are not likely to be disturbed, so that they can be refitted in their original positions when the engine is reassembled; this is important, as in service the ball-ends and cups on the rods become lapped to the tappets and rocker screws with which they mate.

The cylinder head is now ready to be lifted off the cylinder block. Unscrew the nuts progressively in the sequence shown in Fig. 21.

If the head does not come away easily, no attempt should be made to prise it up by inserting a screwdriver or similar tool between the head and the block, as this may damage the machined surfaces. A sharp tap with

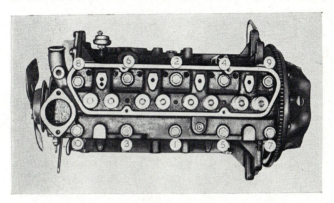

Fig. 21. Sequence in which cylinder head nuts should be progressively tightened or slackened

a wooden mallet, or with a hammer on a block of wood held against the side of the head, should free the joint.

Remove the manifolds and put the various parts aside for later attention.

Removing Cylinder Heads from V4 Engines. The items which obstruct removal of the inlet manifold and cylinder heads must first be taken off. Among the major units are the dynamo, ignition distributor (*see* pages 66–7), the air cleaner and carburettor and the thermostat housing and thermostat.

When the top of the engine has been cleared for action, unbolt the exhaust manifold flanges and take off the rocker covers. Notice that the right-hand cover incorporates the oil filler neck and that the left cover has a baffle and a crankcase fume-emission valve.

The inlet manifold is an aluminium casting. The retaining nuts should therefore be undone progressively to avoid distortion, in the order shown in Fig. 22.

The rocker retaining nuts can now be undone and the rockers and push-rods removed, keeping each pair together and laying them out in the sequence in which they are fitted to the engine. Take off the forked rocker guide plates.

The cylinder heads are now ready to be removed, again slackening the nuts progressively in the sequence shown in Fig. 22 to avoid distortion. The cylinder heads can now be lifted off, as described for in-line engines.

Decarbonizing the Pistons. Rotate the crankshaft by pulling on the fan belt until two of the pistons are at the tops of the cylinders. Stuff clean rags into the bores of the remaining two cylinders and in the push-rod openings, the water-ways and the oil-feed drilling in the cylinder block.

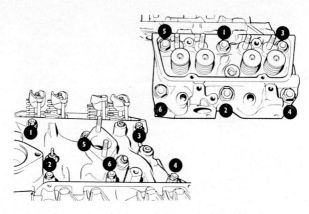

Fig. 22. Sequence of tightening cylinder-head bolts (above) and inlet manifold nuts (below) on V4 engines

Remove the carbon from the piston crowns with a suitable blunt scraper, taking care not to score the surfaces. Then burnish the crowns with a wire brush. Do not use an abrasive, such as metal polish, owing to the risk of particles being trapped in the piston ring grooves or between the rings and the cylinder walls.

Most authorities recommend that a narrow ring of carbon should be left around the edge of the piston crown, and that the ring around the top of the cylinder bore should not be disturbed; these can form a useful oil seal if the piston rings and bores are no longer in perfect condition. This is where an old piston ring comes into the picture: placed on top of the piston, it provides a mask to protect the carbon seals from the scraper and the wire brush.

Decarbonizing the Cylinder Head and Valves. It is best to decarbonize the cylinder head or heads before removing the valves. Any risk of damaging the valve seatings will then be avoided. Scrape off every trace of carbon and burnish the surfaces with a wire brush; a cup-shaped brush, used in the chuck of an electric drill, is ideal for this job but patient hand work will give equally good results. Clean the gasket face of the head, taking particular care not to score it.

The valves can now be removed. The best tool to use to compress the valve springs is the official service compressor. If this is not available, shape a piece of wood to fit a combustion chamber and place the head over this on the bench, so that the heads of the valves rest against the wood. The spring cap can then be forced downwards by applying pressure with the tips of a pair of screwdrivers, and held in this position by one screwdriver, allowing the spring cap to tilt and jam against the stem, while the cotters are removed. As already mentioned, however, the cotters are more easily taken out if a valve-spring compressor is used to compress the springs.

Discard the valve springs if, as recommended earlier, a new set is to be fitted. Otherwise stand them in line on a level surface and discard any that are noticeably shorter than the others or which have distorted coils.

As each valve is withdrawn from its guide it should be placed in the correct order on the bench. The valves should not be interchanged. It is a good plan to drill holes in a length of wood or punch a strip of card-board to take the stems and to number these to correspond with the positions in the head.

The undersides of the valve heads, the stems and the ports in the head, which could not be reached when the valves were in position, should now be thoroughly cleaned. Care must be taken not to score the seatings of the valves and the combustion chambers.

The valve stems should be scraped clean. Emery cloth should not be used on the sections that work in the guides. The guides themselves should be cleaned out by drawing a paraffin-soaked rag through them. Each valve should then be checked for fit in its own guide. Any noticeable degree of sideways shake indicates the need for new valves and, possibly, reconditioning of the guides.

Modern Ford engines are unusual in that the valve guides are machined directly in the cylinder head, instead of being inserted separately. To compensate for wear in the guides, valves which have stems 3-thousandths or 5-thousandths of an inch oversize are available but in practice replacements are seldom needed during the service life of the engine. However, if the 3-thousandths oversize does not take up the wear, it will be necessary to have the valve guide bores reamed out to take the larger stems. This calls for careful and precise work. The cylinder-head should therefore be taken to the local Ford dealer, who will not only open-out the guides but will recut the valve seatings, using special equipment. It is useless to grind-in the valves when the stems and guides are worn, or to fit oversize valves, without recutting the seatings in the cylinder head.

In any case, if the seatings on the valves and in the cy inder head are badly pitted, it will be necessary to recut them with special abrasive stones and to true-up the valve faces in a suitable machine. Excessive grinding-in, in an attempt to remove deep pitting, merely results in recessed seatings and incorrect mating angles, which cause loss of power. It is then necessary to use a special cutter to narrow the seatings, followed by the normal reseating.

It should not be necessary to dismantle the rocker assembly of an in-line engine unless there appears to be excessive play between the rockers

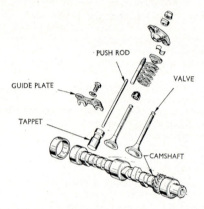

Fig. 23. The valve gear assembly of a V4 engine

and the shaft. In such a case ask your local Ford dealer's advice about reconditioning the parts or fitting replacements.

On V4 engines the rockers and the self-locking nuts should also be serviceable—but if the nuts have become a slack fit on the studs, it may be difficult to maintain the correct valve clearance. If the threads on the rocker studs are damaged or if the studs are bent or broken, your Ford dealer can install oversize replacements. The studs are a press fit in the head and to do the job properly it is essential to use special service tools.

Grinding-in the Valves. If the valves and seatings are in good condition, or have received the appropriate treatment as described above, the next step is to grind-in—or, more correctly, lap-in—each valve on to its seating in order to obtain a gas-tight seal.

The inlet valves on the Cortina cross-flow and the V4 engines, however, are exceptions to the general rule. Their faces are given a special diffused aluminium coating to increase their resistance to high-temperature oxidization and to form a hard, wear-resistant surface on the seating area.

These properties will be destroyed if the aluminium surface is ground away by lapping the valve on to its seating. If the seatings in the cylinder head are pitted a Ford dealer will be able to true them up with a special cutter, or the job can be done at home by using a spare new valve and grinding compound, as described below.

If the seating faces of the valves are worn or pitted, new valves must be installed and the seatings in the cylinder head must be trued-up with a cutter or a "slave" valve as just described.

Fig. 24. Grinding-in valve

The suction tool 1 is spun between the palms to lap the valve 2 lightly on to its seating

Valve-grinding paste is usually supplied in two grades, fine and coarse, in one container. The coarse grade should be used only in an emergency, to remove deep pitting when proper reconditioning cannot be carried out. Light pitting may be removed with the fine paste until a good matt finish has been obtained.

Each valve should be rotated quickly and lightly with the suction-cup grinding tool, first in one direction and then in the other, spinning the handle of the tool between the palms of the hands. From time to time raise the valve from its seat and turn it a quarter of a turn. This will ensure that an even, concentric surface is obtained. Only a light downward pressure is required on the valve.

When correctly ground, the valve seat and the face of the valve should have an even, clean, grey matt finish with no signs of bright rings or any evidence of pitting. Bright rings are caused by grinding with insufficient grinding paste, while "tramlines" are usually the result of continuously grinding the valve on its seat without taking up a different position.

Check the effectiveness of the seal by making a series of pencil marks across the face of the valve with a soft lead pencil. Replace the valve and rotate it once through a quarter of a turn on its seating. If the valve is seating properly, each pencil mark should be erased at the line of contact. If some of the lines are not broken, the indication is that either the valve or its seating is not truly circular and that renewal or refacing of the valve or seat (or both) is required.

When all the valves have been ground-in the valves and seatings should be thoroughly cleaned and all traces of grinding paste removed with a clean cloth and a little petrol. Lubricate the valve stems with a little clean engine oil before refitting the valves in their correct positions and reassembling the springs and retainers. Make sure that the inverted oil-sealing cup, the valve-spring cap and each pair of cotters are correctly seated on the valve stem.

Replacing the Cylinder Head on In-line Engines. Before refitting the cylinder head make sure that the piston crowns, cylinder walls and the top of the block are scrupulously clean. Pour a small quantity of engine oil around each bore so that it will be distributed over the cylinder walls and down the sides of the pistons when the engine is first turned over.

It is important to line-up the gasket and cylinder head accurately with the bolt-holes in the cylinder block and this can best be done by screwing "slave" studs in diagonally-opposite holes at the front and rear of the block. These studs can be obtained from a Ford dealer or can be made by cutting the head off a bolt and slotting the end to take a screwdriver, so that the studs can be unscrewed and replaced by bolts when the head has been fitted.

The new cylinder-head gasket should be smeared on both faces with high-melting-point grease and located over the bolt holes in the cylinder block. Place the head in position and fit the bolts. First screw them down finger-tight and then tighten them *progressively and evenly* in the order shown in Fig. 21. Tighten them firmly with a spanner of normal length. Do not be tempted to apply extra leverage.

Place the eight push-rods in position, making sure that they locate in their respective tappets, and place the rocker-shaft assembly on the studs. Carefully work it into position, making sure that the rocker-adjusting screws engage properly in the push-rod cups. Tighten the bolts down evenly.

Adjust the valve clearances as described on pages 27–30. The remainder of the reassembly is quite straightforward. After a final check all round, refill the cooling system and start the engine. If a heater is fitted, check the level of the water in the header tank after the engine has been running for a few minutes. When the engine is well warmed-up, switch off and go over the cylinder-head and manifold nuts again. The nuts should be checked a second time after about 200 miles' running. Remember to readjust the valve clearances on each occasion, as they will be reduced when the cylinder head is pulled down.

When the engine has been decarbonized, the ignition timing should be checked as described in Chapter 7. It is usually possible to advance the ignition slightly. Also, the carburettor slow-running mixture strength and speed will usually require readjustment, as described in Chapter 6.

Replacing the Cylinder Heads on V4 Engines. When replacing the cylinder heads on V4 engines the procedure is similar to that just described but the following points must be remembered—

A pair of "slave" locating studs will facilitate accurate lining-up of each head, as described for in-line engines.

Identical gaskets are used for each cylinder head, made of a composition material, reinforced with copper around the cylinder bores. The inlet manifold gasket is also of a composition material, but has cork inserts at both ends to form oil-tight joints between the manifold and the front and rear walls of the cylinder block tappet chamber. The ends of the gasket must be trimmed flush with the rocker cover mounting faces after the manifold has been fitted. Tighten the bolts progressively, working from the front and rear inwards (Fig. 22), and check the tightness again when the engine has been brought up to operating temperature—but only after the cylinder head nuts have been tightened down.

Do not forget to fit the push-rod guide plates. Place each rocker over its stud, insert the push-rod and screw down the retaining nut.

The method of adjusting the valve clearances is described on pages 27–30. If the engine is run with the rocker covers removed (for example to check for a noisy tappet) the emission valve must be connected to the inlet manifold. Otherwise the carburettor mixture strength will be excessively weakened.

6 The carburettor and fuel pump

ALTHOUGH the carburettors fitted to these cars are somewhat complex (but very efficient) instruments, maintenance and adjustment should be well within the capabilities of most readers. This applies, of course, specifically to routine jobs; carburettor tuning, as such, calls for a considerable degree of experience and know-how. It is best not to interfere with the standard jet settings. Departures from normal, in fact, will be needed only in exceptional circumstances—for example, when the car is operating at high altitudes or under other abnormal conditions. In such cases the local Ford dealer will have the latest factory service information available.

When describing carburettor servicing and adjustments, we shall be dealing with a number of different types of carburettor. A Zenith carburettor similar to that shown in Fig. 25 is used on the Cortina 1500, the early Corsair which has an in-line-port engine, and the 1340 c.c. and 1500 c.c. Classic.

The Corsair V4 de Luxe has a single-venturi Zenith carburettor similar to that shown in Fig. 28 while the 2000 and 2000E have double-choke Weber carburettors (Fig. 32). The earlier Corsair GT had a single-barrel Solex.

The Cortina 1200 c.c. engine has a Solex carburettor similar to Fig. 26, and the later, cross-flow Cortina 1300 and 1600 engines, single-barrel Ford carburettors (Figs. 29 and 31). The 1500 GT and 1600 GT have a double-barrel Weber (Figs. 27 and 32).

When an automatic transmission is fitted to these cars, the carburettor is provided with an automatic choke which is operated by a thermostatic spring in a housing which is heated by water drawn from the engine cooling system. This choke should not be dismantled. If its operation is upset, cold starting, the operation of the engine during the warming-up period and the fuel consumption will be adversely affected.

Cleaning the Jets. The filter gauze fitted to the bowl of the fuel pump is sufficiently fine to render it unlikely that grit or water will find its way into the carburettor float chamber but very fine particles of sediment do eventually accumulate in the base of the chamber and the possibility of a choked jet cannot be entirely ignored. It is advisable to forestall trouble, therefore, by occasionally removing the float chamber, flushing out any

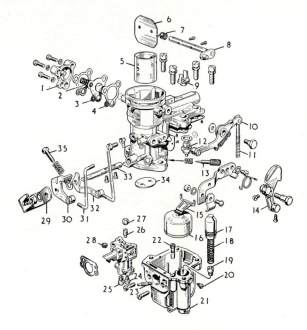

Fig. 25. Earlier type of Zenith carburettor

1. *Economy valve cover*
2. *Economy valve spring*
3. *Economy valve diaphragm*
4. *Diaphragm gasket*
5. *Choke tube or venturi*
6. *Air strangler (choke) flap*
7. *Air strangler spring*
8. *Air strangler lever*
9. *Accelerator pump stroke adjuster*
10. *Accelerator pump lever*
11. *Pump spring*
12. *Needle valve*
13. *Volume-control screw*
14. *Strangler control lever*
15. *Float lever*
16. *Float*
17. *Accelerator pump piston*
18. *Pump spring*

19. *Pump check valve*
20. *Pump piston stop screw*
21. *Float chamber or bowl*
22. *Pump discharge valve*
23. *Pump jet*
24. *Compensating jet*
25. *Main jet*
26. *Slow-running jet*
27. *Air bleed screw*
28. *Ventilation screw*
29. *Throttle lever*
30. *Throttle stop*
31. *Pump link*
32. *Interconnecting lever and rod*
33. *Throttle spindle*
34. *Throttle plate*
35. *Throttle stop-screw*

sediment and removing the jets and blowing through them and the jet passages to ensure that they are clear. For this purpose it is possible to obtain from accessory dealers a useful conical rubber nozzle that can be fitted to the connector of a tyre pump.

On the Zenith carburettor shown in Fig. 25, support the float-chamber bowl with the hand, unscrew the four retaining screws, lower the bowl, at the same time moving it away from the carburettor, and invert it to remove the float and float lever, both of which are marked for correct assembly. The slow-running jet is the most likely to be blocked. To obtain access to it it is necessary to unscrew the air bleed screw (No. 27, Fig. 25). The jet can then be removed with a screwdriver.

The main and compensating jets are in the base of the emulsion block, from which the spraying beak protrudes through the side of the float-chamber bowl. The block can be removed by undoing the two retaining screws. It is impossible to replace the two jets incorrectly since the thread of the main jet is of larger diameter than that of the compensating jet. When refitting the block, do not omit the gasket between the block and the bowl.

The positions of the jets in the Zenith carburettor fitted to V4 engines can be seen in Fig. 28. It will be necessary to remove the upper casting and the emulsion block before they can be removed and cleaned. It is advisable to fit a new float chamber gasket unless the condition of the original gasket is beyond suspicion.

Before discussing the jets in the Weber carburettor it should be explained that these carburettors are unusual in having two choke tubes (or venturis), each with its associated jet system, and two throttles, thus providing, in effect, twin carburettors mounted in a common body and fed from a single float chamber.

This arrangement has several advantages over the conventional twin-carburettor arrangement used on the majority of sports car engines. In the first place the problem of accurately synchronizing two carburettors does not arise. Secondly, in this Weber design the two throttles do not open simultaneously. Instead, the initial movement of the accelerator pedal opens only the primary throttle, which is provided with a size of venturi and jet settings which ensure good pick-up from low speeds and economical cruising under part-throttle conditions. The second venturi comes into action only when greater power is required. By an ingenious cam linkage the secondary throttle is arranged to open at a quicker rate than the primary, so that by the time that the accelerator is fully depressed, both throttles are fully open. Under these conditions the "breathing" capacity of a conventional twin-carburettor system is provided.

As will be seen from Fig. 27 the primary and secondary idling and main jets are accessible by unscrewing plugs from the exterior of the carburettor body. In the case of the carburettor shown in Fig. 32, the main jets are in the base of the float chamber. To remove these, and any of the other jest in both types of carburettor, the float needle valve or the accelerator

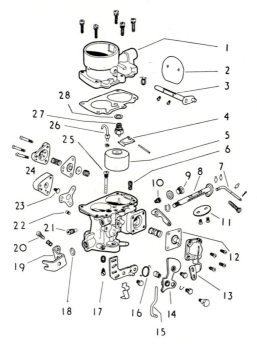

Fig. 26. Solex carburettor fitted to 1,200 c.c. Cortina

1. Float-chamber cover
2. Choke flap
3. Choke spindle
4. Float lever
5. Float
6. Anti-siphon valve
7. Pump control rod
8. Throttle spindle
9. Main jet plug
10. Main jet
11. Throttle disc
12. Acceleration pump diaphragm
13. Acceleration pump cover and lever
14. Choke cam

15. Fast-idle interconnexion rod
16. Choke cam return screw
17. Idling mixture control spring
18. Throttle spindle seal
19. Throttle lever
20. Slow-running speed adjustment
21. Slow-running jet
22. Economy jet
23. Economy valve
24. Economy-valve cover, body and diaphragm
25. Emulsion tube
26. Acceleration pump injector tube
27. Float needle valve
28. Needle valve washer

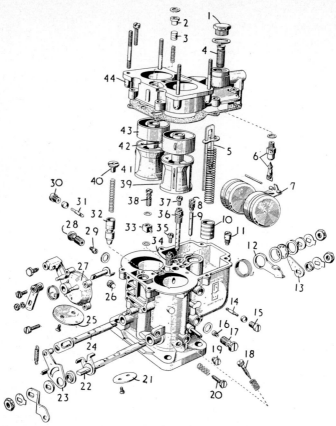

Fig. 27. Weber carburettor fitted to earlier GT models, except V4

1. Filter plug
2. Starter plunger seat
3. Starter plunger
4. Filter
5. Pump-operating rod
6. Needle valve and seating
7. Float lever
8. Starting air jet
9. Starting jet
10. Pump plunger
11. Pump intake valve
12. Pump-operating lever
13. Pump-operating cam
14. Primary idling jet
15. Primary idling jet holder
16. Primary main jet
17. Primary main jet holder
18. Idling mixture adjusting screw
19. Progression hole inspection screw
20. Idling speed adjusting screw
21. Primary throttle
22. Primary throttle shaft
23. Primary sector
24. Secondary throttle shaft
25. Secondary throttle
26. Progression hole inspection screw
27. Starting control
28. Secondary main jet holder
29. Secondary main jet
30. Secondary idling jet holder
31. Secondary idling jet
32. Starting valve
33. Pump jet
34. Secondary emulsion tube
35. Secondary air correction jet
36. Primary emulsion tube
37. Primary air correction jet
38. Pump delivery valve
39. Primary choke
40. Starting spring guide
41. Secondary choke
42. Primary auxiliary venturi
43. Secondary auxiliary venturi
44. Carburettor top casting

pump plunger and non-return valves, the upper casting of the carburettor must be taken off.

On Weber carburettors, unscrew the plug which retains the fuel filter. This is shown in Figs. 27 and 32. Remove the gauze filter and swill it in petrol.

Turning now to the Solex carburettor (Fig. 26), the main, slow-running and economy jets can be removed without dismantling the carburettor but the upper casting must be taken off if attention is required to the float needle valve, emulsion tube, or anti-siphon valve.

Jets should be cleaned by washing them in petrol and blowing through them in the reverse direction to the normal flow of fuel. Never use wire to probe them. They are calibrated to very fine limits and engine performance and economy will suffer if these orifices are altered. The jets are clearly numbered—the greater the number the larger the jet.

When refitting the upper body of a Ford carburettor to the lower body, connect the choke link to the fast-idle cam while fitting the upper body, and position the manual choke cable bracket beneath the rear retaining screw. Tighten the retaining screw while holding the choke lever in the closed position. If this is not done the lever will be over-centre and the choke will not operate. *Do not force the lever back to the correct position;* instead, slacken the screws and retighten them while holding the lever in the closed position.

Another important point when dealing with Ford carburettors is that the accelerator pump discharge valve and the small weight which keeps it in position are exposed when the upper part of the carburettor has been removed. If the throttle is opened quickly the valve and weight may be ejected and may roll into the carburettor intake and find their way into the inlet manifold. If this is not noticed and the engine is started, serious damage may be done.

After cleaning the jets the slow-running adjustments should, if necessary, be reset as described on pages 58–60.

Acceleration Pump. All three types of carburettor have an acceleration pump which provides an extra spurt of fuel when the throttle is suddenly depressed. On the Zenith and the Weber carburettors the pump is of the spring-loaded plunger type. To service the plunger and valves it will be necessary to dismantle the carburettors.

Failure of the acceleration pump to deliver sufficient petrol will be reflected in poor acceleration and a "flat spot" when the throttle is suddenly opened. These symptoms will also occur in cold weather, however, if the travel of the pump lever is restricted by adjustment of the linkage to the "Summer" position. On the Zenith carburettor fitted to all except V4 engines there is an adjustable stop beneath the pump lever which can be rotated to bring a long or a short projection beneath the lever. When the movement of the lever is restricted by the longer projection, the supply of fuel during acceleration is cut down and during warm

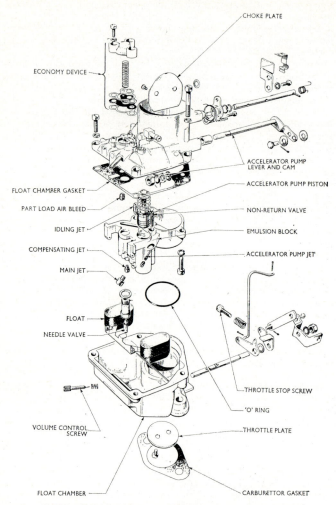

CHOKE PLATE

ECONOMY DEVICE

ACCELERATOR PUMP LEVER AND CAM

FLOAT CHAMBER GASKET

ACCELERATOR PUMP PISTON

PART LOAD AIR BLEED

NON-RETURN VALVE

IDLING JET

EMULSION BLOCK

COMPENSATING JET

ACCELERATOR PUMP JET

MAIN JET

FLOAT

NEEDLE VALVE

THROTTLE STOP SCREW

'O' RING

VOLUME CONTROL SCREW

THROTTLE PLATE

FLOAT CHAMBER

CARBURETTOR GASKET

Fig. 28. Zenith carburettor fitted to earlier V4 engines

weather the output of the pump can be reduced in this manner without sacrifice of performance and with a corresponding gain in petrol economy but in the winter the block should be rotated so that the shorter projection is beneath the lever, thus allowing a longer travel of the pump piston.

On the Zenith carburettor fitted to V4 engines there are two holes in the pump operating lever. If the pivot pin at the upper end of the throttle link is inserted in the lower hole, the pump stroke is restricted. This is the "Summer" setting. The upper hole provides a longer stroke and is thus the normal setting for cold weather. Fit a washer on each side of the pump lever and link before replacing the split pin.

On the Weber carburettor the stroke of the pump-operating lever is not adjustable. On the Solex design, the pump pull-rod is normally fitted in the lower hole in the flange of the pump-operating lever. This gives good economy with adequate power. The upper hole provides an increased delivery from the pump. It might be worth trying this position if hesitant acceleration is experienced in cold weather.

Float and Needle Valve. The level of the fuel in the float chamber can exercise a considerable influence on carburation. Normally no attempt should be made to alter the level but if it is suspected that it is too high, as shown by difficulty in obtaining a satisfactory tick-over, accompanied by black smoke from the exhaust and possibly a smell of petrol in the car, the float-operated needle valve in the upper casting of the carburettor should be unscrewed and swilled in petrol. Sometimes a particle of grit will become lodged on the valve, but the more usual trouble, after a considerable mileage, is slight ridging of the faces of the valve and its seating. If cleaning the valve does not rectify matters, always fit a replacement valve and seating as a complete assembly.

Another possible cause of too high a petrol level when a hollow float is fitted is a punctured float. If the float is immersed in hot water even a pinhole leak can be detected by the emergence of bubbles as the petrol vapour inside the float expands. Although it is possible to seal a small leak with a spot of solder, a more satisfactory cure is to renew the float.

When twin floats are fitted, make sure that the connecting bar is not distorted (the floats must be parallel and at the same height) and check that the tongue which operates the needle valve has not been bent, as this would cause an incorrect fuel level.

If the foregoing attentions are still ineffective, the most likely trouble is the development of excessive pressure by the fuel pump. It is as well to ask a Ford dealer to check the pressure with a special gauge.

Float-chamber Gaskets. The float chamber bowl gaskets should be in perfect condition, both to prevent petrol leakage and to ensure that the economy device described in the next section will operate satisfactorily.

When the carburettor has been reassembled the idling speed and mixture strength should be checked and adjusted as described on pages 58–60.

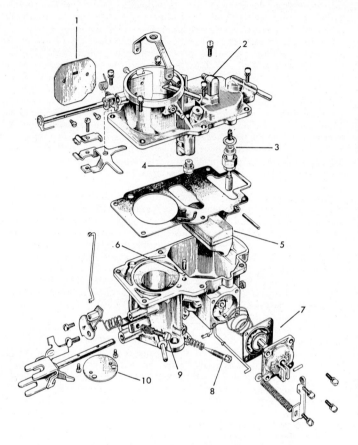

Fig. 29. Ford carburettor fitted to later Cortina engines

1. *Choke flap*
2. *Float-chamber vent*
3. *Float needle-valve assembly*
4. *Main jet*
5. *Float*

6. *Accelerator pump ball valve*
7. *Accelerator pump*
8. *Idling-mixture volume control*
9. *Throttle-stop screw*
10. *Throttle plate*

Economy Device. The Zenith and Solex carburettors each have an economy device which provides a weaker mixture than normal under part-throttle cruising conditions, when a rather "lean" mixture can be burnt without the risk of overheating the valves, sparking plugs or piston crowns. On the Zenith, a small cover, attached to the side of the carburettor by three screws, contains a spring-loaded diaphragm valve that seals an extra air passage. The interior of the cover is connected by a drilling in the carburettor to the engine side of the throttle, so that it is subject to the fluctuating vacuum in the inlet manifold.

When the engine is running under part-throttle conditions this vacuum is sufficiently high to draw the diaphragm back against the spring pressure,

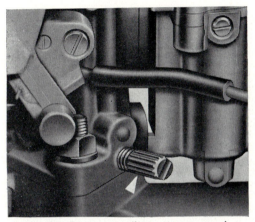

Fig. 30. Carburettor idling mixture control

The volume-control screw indicated by the arrow controls the slow-running mixture strength on Zenith carburettors. A similar adjustment is used on Ford, Solex and Weber models. This and the throttle-stop screw are shown in the illustrations in this chapter

thus allowing air to pass through the air bleed and weaken the mixture.

The device needs no attention, apart from renewal of the diaphragm after a very long period of service. If the cover is removed, fit new gaskets on each side of the diaphragm and make sure that the screws are firmly tightened. Obviously, an air leak at the cover will put the device out of action. It is also important to prevent air leakage at the junction between the float-chamber bowl and the carburettor body, as emphasized in the preceding section.

On the Solex carburettor the economy device operates in the opposite sense to the Zenith design. Under part-throttle conditions the normal main jet provides a weak mixture; meanwhile the economy device, which consists, like the Zenith, of a vacuum-operated diaphragm, is withdrawn against spring pressure, sucking petrol into the diaphragm housing. When the throttle is opened the vacuum is reduced and the spring returns the diaphragm, allowing petrol to flow from the economy unit to the engine. When the reserve in the diaphragm housing is used up, flow continues through the metering jet for as long as the extra fuel supply is needed to prevent the engine overheating and to allow maximum power to be developed.

Slow-running Adjustments. Most engines are very sensitive to carburettor slow-running adjustments; an adjustment which gives a perfect "tick-over" on one engine may not do so on another of exactly the same type.

The strength of the slow-running mixture considerably influences acceleration from low speeds. If there is a "flat-spot" when the throttle is opened from the idling position, try the effect of slightly enriching the slow-running mixture as described below; a fraction of a turn of the screw may be sufficient. It will probably be necessary to adjust the stop screw slightly to prevent "lumpy" idling, but an idling setting that is slightly on the rich side is an advantage.

Remember that it will be impossible to obtain good idling if ignition or mechanical faults exist.

The throttle stop-screw controls the amount by which the throttle approaches the closed position and therefore regulates the slow-running speed. The richness of the slow-running mixture is determined by the volume-control screw, a greater volume of mixture being admitted when the screw is turned anticlockwise.

To obtain the exact settings the engine should be at normal running temperature and the throttle stop-screw turned so that the engine will run fast enough to prevent stalling. The volume-adjusting screw should then be screwed in or out until the engine runs evenly. The throttle stop-screw should now be readjusted if the engine is running too fast, followed by a further adjustment of the volume-adjusting screw. The operations should be repeated until satisfactory idling is obtained.

While the above instructions are substantially the same as those given in most handbooks, some amplification may be desirable for the benefit of the novice. For example, how does one judge whether the mixture is too rich or too weak?

Experiment first by turning the volume-control screw in an anticlockwise direction to enrich the mixture, until the idling becomes unsteady and the engine runs with a rhythmic beat. If the mixture is enriched beyond this point the exhaust will show puffs of dark smoke and the exhaust gas will have a characteristic sweet smell. Next, screw the control inwards until the engine passes through the smooth idling range and begins to misfire slightly. The exhaust will now have a "splashy" note and the gas will be odourless.

Midway between these points will be the ideal slow-running mixture.

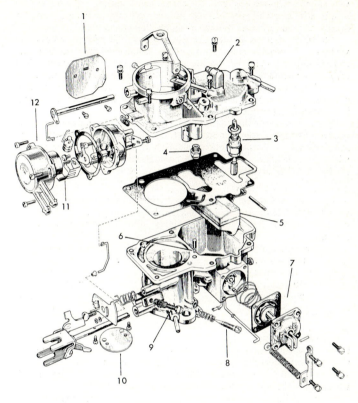

Fig. 31. Automatic-choke version of Ford carburettor

1. Choke flap
2. Float-chamber vent
3. Float needle-valve assembly
4. Main jet
5. Float
6. Pump ball valve
7. Accelerator pump
8. Idling-mixture volume control
9. Throttle-stop screw
10. Throttle plate
11. Thermostatic spring
12. Water-heated choke housing

In practice, however, it is better to set the carburettor with the mixture very slightly rich—that is, with the engine just "hunting" slightly—as this setting will give the best pick-up on snap throttle openings from low speeds, without appreciably increasing the fuel consumption.

If the mixture is set on the weak side, not only will there be a hesitation when the throttle is snapped open but explosions may occur in the exhaust system when the throttle is closed at fairly high speeds. This trouble, incidentally, will be aggravated by air leakage at any point in the system. It should be rectified as soon as possible, not only in order to cure the noise but also because there is a risk of the silencer being split if a particularly violent explosion should occur.

Finally, remember that with modern engines, one should not expect to obtain a very slow and even idling setting. It is better to keep the idling speed slightly on the high side, particularly if the engine is worn, as there will be less likelihood of the plugs becoming oiled-up during long periods of idling in traffic and the engine will accelerate better from very low speeds.

Fast-idling Adjustment. On some carburettors there is an adjustment at the upper end of the rod that connects the choke to the throttle, opening the latter slightly and providing a higher idling speed when the choke is in use.

In practice it is usually possible to achieve a satisfactory setting of the lever by trial-and-error methods, the object being to obtain an idling speed which is sufficiently high to prevent the engine stalling when the choke is in use, but which will not cause the engine to race when the choke control is pulled out fully, or hold the throttle slightly open when the choke control is pushed home.

Carburettor Tuning. The jets fitted as standard will give the best results under all normal running conditions, including operation at altitudes of up to 5,000 ft. Alternative settings will be necessary when the car is consistently run at higher altitudes and the advice of the local Ford dealer, who will be familiar with local conditions, should be sought.

Owners of earlier 1,340 c.c. models, however, sometimes complain of a slight flat-spot when the throttle is opened fully at low speeds. This was overcome on later cars by a modification in the emulsion block and pump stop. The modified parts can be fitted, if preferred, to earlier carburettors. Alternatively, you can tune-out the flat spot by fitting a size 60 slow-running jet, which provides a slightly richer mixture from the progression holes in the carburettor barrel which are uncovered as the throttle opens. The idling mixture must be readjusted by means of the volume-control screw to compensate for the richer mixture as previously explained.

Sometimes, however, the flat-spot is caused by an unvented float chamber top. A modified replacement will cure the trouble. Another possible cause on early cars is a clogged jet caused by small particles

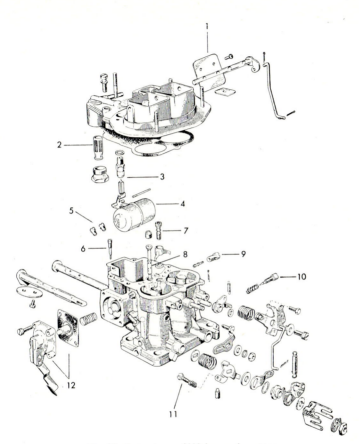

Fig. 32. Later type of Weber carburettor

1. Choke flap
2. Fuel filter
3. Float needle-valve
4. Float
5. Main jets
6. Pump restrictor

7. Pump delivery valve
8. Emulsion tube
9. Idling jet
10. Idling-mixture volume control
11. Throttle-stop screw
12. Accelerator pump

flaking off the internal coating of the fuel feed pipe. If frequent cleaning out of the float chamber and jets is necessary, fit a fuel pipe of the latest type.

THE PETROL PUMP

Provided that the filter is cleaned at regular intervals as described in Chapter 4, the mechanically-operated petrol pump should seldom give trouble. These units have a very long life between overhauls, and when a replacement is eventually needed a service exchange scheme, mentioned later, is available.

If the pump should fail to deliver petrol to the carburettor, check that fuel is available in the tank and that the unions in the pipe connecting the tank to the pump are tight. Also see that the pump filter is clean, that the gasket below or above the filter cover is in good condition and that the clamping screw is firmly tightened. An air leak at the gasket is the most frequent cause of pump failure.

If, after extended service, trouble is experienced with the pump, it is not advisable to attempt to repair it without special equipment. The most satisfactory course is to take advantage of the service-exchange scheme operated by Ford dealers, under which a reconditioned pump can be fitted at quite a modest cost. The dealer will also be able to test the pressure developed by the pump and the rate of fuel flow, with the aid of a special test kit. In this respect it should be remembered that the number of gaskets fitted between the pump and the mounting flange on the crankcase will affect the pressure developed. Also, the retaining nuts must be kept tight, to prevent an oil leak at the flange.

On the V4 engines the fuel system is of the recirculatory type. A return pipe is fitted between the fuel pump and the fuel tank. Some of the fuel supplied by the pump maintains the correct level in the float chamber but any which is surplus to the engine's requirements returns to the tank

7 Servicing the ignition system

FEW owners fully appreciate the extent to which the ignition system affects the efficiency and economy of the engine. All too often the sparking plugs, ignition distributor, coil and so on, function uncomplainingly for months at a time with only superficial service—if any! It is not until misfiring sets in or the car fails to start, that a comprehensive ignition overhaul is put in hand.

Apart from normal routine maintenance, at about 12,000-mile intervals (or, say, once a year) it is as well to have the ignition system thoroughly checked by a garage which has a motorized test panel, on which the efficiency of each component can be quickly assessed and the engine subsequently tuned for maximum performance and fuel economy.

This does not imply, however, that you cannot carry out normal routine servicing yourself. No specialized knowledge is needed; it is simply a matter of following the instructions carefully and renewing any doubtful parts. In this chapter, therefore, it is proposed to deal with straightforward servicing jobs for the benefit of practically-minded owners, in rather greater detail than is possible in the ordinary manufacturer's instruction book.

The Sparking Plugs. First, the sparking plugs. The rules for maximum efficiency can be summed up briefly: fit the correct type of plugs; service them at regular intervals—at least every 6,000 miles, and more frequently if the engine is no longer in first-class condition—and renew them while they still have a reasonable remaining lease of life. Keeping plugs in use until they are completely worn out is an expensive form of economy.

When plug trouble does develop, try to arrive at the basic cause before blaming the plugs themselves. Retarded ignition timing, overheating, excessive oil consumption or a weak carburettor mixture are some of the factors that can affect plug performance.

An owner who indulges in continuous high-speed driving may find that the normal grade of plug has a tendency to overheat, causing pinking, misfiring at full throttle and rapid burning of the electrodes. The same may apply, to a lesser degree, if long spells of driving in low gear are necessary when climbing mountain passes. A "cooler" grade of plug which is able to withstand the greater amount of heat developed under these conditions is the obvious answer.

Much "local" driving, on the other hand, entailing frequent stopping and starting, may cause excessive carbon deposits on ordinary plugs, indicating the need for a "hotter" grade of plug which will burn them off. This also applies if the engine is worn and an excessive amount of oil is reaching the combustion chambers. A "hotter" plug can also be fitted when high-octane fuels are used.

Recommended grades of sparking plugs are given in Chapter 1. The grades for other makes can be ascertained by consulting the lists issued by the plug manufacturers.

Cleaning and Inspecting Sparking Plugs. The plug spanner must be handled carefully to avoid cracking the insulator. Make sure that it fits securely over the plug. After unscrewing the plugs see that the sealing washers do not fall off and become lost.

The usual garage plug cleaner, in which a high-pressure air blast carries a fine abrasive into the interior of the plug, effectively scouring the insulator, the inner walls and points, gives the best results. A useful tip, known to plug specialists, is to true-up the sides of the electrodes lightly with a small, fine-cut file, restoring the sharp corners that existed when the plug was new. This will considerably reduce the voltage needed to produce a spark across the gap.

Adjusting the Plug Gaps. After the plugs have been cleaned and the points trued-up, the gap should be adjusted by bending only the side electrode. One of the inexpensive combination gauges and setting tools sold by plug manufacturers is a worthwhile investment. If an improvised method is used, be careful not to exert leverage against the central electrode; otherwise the internal insulator will probably be cracked, rendering the plug useless.

Refitting the Plugs. The threaded portion of each plug should be cleaned with a stiff brush and a smear of graphite grease placed on the threads. This will ensure that the plug will tighten down easily and will facilitate subsequent removal.

Make sure that the sealing washers are not flattened and screw the plugs home by hand, using the plug spanner only for the final half-turn to ensure a gas-tight joint. Over-tightening is unnecessary and likely to lead to trouble. If the plugs cannot be screwed in by hand, ask the local garage to clean-up the threads in the cylinder head with a plug thread tap.

The Distributor. Working back through the ignition system we come to the distributor, which not only distributes the high-tension current to the sparking plugs but also includes a contact-breaker that interrupts the low-voltage current passing from the battery through the ignition coil; it also (as described in more detail later) has automatic timing devices

DIAGNOSING SPARKING-PLUG TROUBLES

	Plug Condition	Possible Cause	Remedy
Insulator: Body:	Clean, coloured straw to coffee Light carbon deposit	Plug condition correct	
Insulator: Body:	Fluffy grey deposit Fluffy grey deposit	Plug condition correct Deposit due to premium petrol	Clean and reset plugs
Insulator: Body:	Clean, coloured straw or coffee Hard carbon deposits	Too much oil Unsuitable oil Too much upper-cylinder lubricant	Check piston rings and valve guides Check level of oil in sump Reduce upper-cylinder lubricant
Insulator: Electrodes: Body:	Clean, white or pale Partly worn (after short service) Clean	Plug too hot Carburettor mixture too lean Ignition too far advanced	Fit cooler plug Adjust carburettor for richer mixture Retard spark
Insulator: Body:	Sooted-up Sooty	Mixture too rich Ignition too far retarded Plug too cool	Check for excessive use of choke Adjust carburettor for leaner mixture Advance ignition timing Fit hotter plug
Insulator: Body:	Sooted- and oiled-up Sooted- and oiled-up	Plug too cool Too much oil Mixture too rich	Fit hotter plug Adjust carburettor for leaner mixture Check piston-rings Check for too much oil in sump Reduce upper-cylinder lubricant
Insulator:	Cracked inside	Damaged during electrode adjustment Plug too hot Mixture too lean	Fit new plug, adjust gap by bending side electrode only Fit cooler plug Adjust carburettor for richer mixture
Insulator: Electrodes:	Dark, blistered, cracked or partly glazed Badly eroded	Plug too hot for premium petrol	Fit, cooler plug for use with premium petrol

that vary the timing of the sparks at the plugs to suit the engine running conditions at any moment, as described on pages 74–5.

Most instruction manuals dismiss the all-important subject of contact-breaker maintenance far too briefly. It cannot be too strongly emphasized, for example, that the gap between the contact-breaker points should never be measured with a feeler gauge unless the points have previously been trued-up with a fine carborundum stone or with very fine emery

Fig. 33. Ignition distributor and high-tension leads

1. *Snap-on sparking plug connector*
2. *High-tension connexion*
3. *Spring clip*
4. *Distributor cover*
5. *Variable timing adjustment*
6. *Clamping bolt*
7. *Vacuum timing control*
8. *Timing scale*

cloth. After only a few hundred miles of running a small "pip" forms on one point and a corresponding "crater" on the other, owing to the transference of microscopic particles of metal by the spark that occurs whenever the points open. The "pip" renders it impossible to obtain a correct reading with a feeler gauge.

Although the distributor is quite accessible, it is preferable (but not essential) to remove it from the engine for servicing. To avoid upsetting the ignition timing, remove only the setscrew that secures the clamp beneath the distributor to the crankcase. Don't slacken the pinch-bolt that passes through the clamping plate; otherwise the ignition timing will be altered.

It will be necessary to remove the distributor cap, disconnect the low-tension wire from the terminal on the side of the distributor and disconnect the pipe union at the vacuum-timing control, being careful not to twist the small-diameter pipeline. The distributor can then be lifted away.

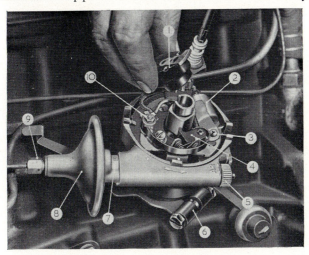

Fig. 34. Ignition distributor with cover removed

1. Rotor
2. Condenser
3. Condenser strap screw
4. Contact-breaker lever
5. Variable timing adjustment
6. Bolt in split clamp locking distributor body
7. Timing scale
8. Vacuum timing control
9. Vacuum pipe connexion
10. Contact-breaker spring terminal post

It will be seen that the projection on the driving coupling is offset, so that it will be impossible to replace the distributor with the rotor pointing in the wrong direction.

Cleaning and Truing the Contacts. To render the contact-breaker points more accessible, pull off the rotor. If it is a tight fit, gentle leverage can be applied with the tip of a screwdriver, taking care not to crack the plastic. The contact-breaker points should have a clean, frosted appearance, apart from the development of the small pip and crater.

If the distributor has not been removed from the engine, a mirror and possibly an inspection light will be useful when examining the points but it is assumed that they will, in any event, be removed from the distributor for closer examination and truing-up.

On the earlier type distributor shown in Figs. 35 and 36, unscrew the nut on the terminal post that retains the end of the contact-arm spring and remove the insulator and both terminal tags. The rocker arm can then be pulled off its pivot. Make a careful note of the position of the insulating sleeve and washers so that they can be reassembled correctly. The fixed contact plate can now be removed by undoing the retaining screw.

Fig. 35. Adjusting gap between contact-breaker points

The gap is varied by rotating a screwdriver blade in the notch 1, after slackening the screw 2, and is measured with a feeler gauge, 3. The rocking lever 4 must be on the crest of one of the "humps" of the cam. A similar adjustment is used on later distributors

On the later types of distributor shown in Fig. 37, it is necessary only to loosen the retaining screw and remove the low-tension and condenser wires from the contact-breaker mechanism, unscrew the retaining and adjusting screws, and lift off the complete contact-breaker assembly.

Adjusting the Contact-breaker Gap. When the contact-breaker points have been trued and reassembled correctly (do not overlook the fibre washers beneath the rocker arm and the anchored end of the spring) the gap should be adjusted. The projection on the fibre block must be exactly on the crest of one of the "humps" of the cam. A slight movement of the cam in either direction will give a false reading—hence the recommendation that adjustment is best carried out with the contact-breaker on the bench.

The screw that retains the fixed contact plate should be slackened and the plate moved by inserting a screwdriver blade in the notch in its edge and turning it clockwise to reduce the gap or anticlockwise to increase it. After tightening the securing screw the gap should be rechecked.

The correct gap between the points of the earlier distributor is 0·014–0·016 in. (14 to 16 thousandths of an inch); a 15-thou. gauge should just slide between them. The later distributor requires a gap of 0·025 in. (25 thousandths of an inch). Again, it is best to check with a slightly undersize and an oversize gauge to make sure that the gap is correct.

The Ignition Condenser. If the contact-breaker points are badly burned the trouble may be due to too small a gap, which will seriously reduce the life of the points. In most cases, however, it is logical to suspect the condenser, which is connected across the contact points in order to absorb the surge of current that builds up in the primary winding of the ignition coil (in addition to the current induced in the high-tension winding), and which, in the absence of a condenser, would cause a destructive arc across the contact-breaker points, instead of the normal slight spark. The condenser also discharges back through the primary windings, causing a more rapid collapse of the magnetic flux and a more intense spark at the sparking plug. It will be obvious, therefore, that an inefficient condenser will not only cause rapid burning of the points but will also result in a weak spark or—if it should short-circuit internally—failure of the plugs to fire at all.

When misfiring and difficult starting are experienced the best test is to substitute a new condenser, or one that is known to be sound. Before finally condemning a condenser make sure that there is no break or short-circuit in the flexible lead connecting it to the contact-breaker terminal post.

Distributor Rotor and Cap. The high-tension current from the coil enters the centre of the distributor cap and passes to the rotor through a spring-loaded brush—actually, a short pencil-shaped length of carbon which also acts as a suppressor to reduce the interference that would otherwise be picked up by nearby radio and television receivers. From the brass tip of the rotor the current jumps in turn to each of the terminals in the distributor cap, to which the sparking plug leads are connected in sequence to give the correct firing order, which on these engines is 1,2,4,3.

The brass contact on the rotor and the terminals inside the cap should be scraped bright and clean. The carbon brush should also be checked. It does not wear away quickly but sometimes tends to stick in its guide. Do not be tempted to overstretch the spring and be careful not to break the brush.

Any accumulation of dust or oily deposits inside the cap, which will tend to attract moisture in damp weather and thus provide a leakage path for the high-tension current, should be removed with petrol and the

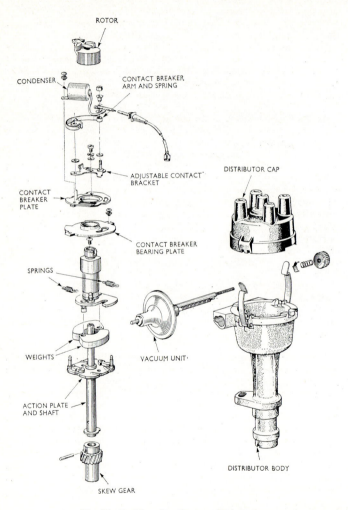

ROTOR

CONDENSER

CONTACT BREAKER
ARM AND SPRING

DISTRIBUTOR CAP

ADJUSTABLE CONTACT
BRACKET

CONTACT
BREAKER
PLATE

CONTACT BREAKER
BEARING PLATE

SPRINGS

WEIGHTS

VACUUM UNIT

ACTION PLATE
AND SHAFT

DISTRIBUTOR BODY

SKEW GEAR

Fig. 36. Ignition distributor of V4 engine

interior surface polished with a clean cloth. If current has been leaking between the terminals, it will have left evidence in the form of dark tracks on the surface of the plastic. Sometimes these can be removed by a thorough cleaning with metal polish but bad "tracking" usually calls for renewal of the cap.

Similarly, the rotor should be thoroughly examined for signs of tracking. Occasionally internal leakage develops from the underside of the brass electrode through the plastic to the interior surface, allowing the high-tension current to jump to the cam spindle and so to earth. Needless to say, this can be a very elusive fault to spot unless one has previously experienced it.

High-tension Leads. On the high-tension side of the ignition system we are dealing with high voltages which will "flash over" or take the line of least resistance whenever possible. The high-tension leads between the coil and the distributor and between the distributor cap and the sparking plugs must, therefore, be tested at intervals by doubling the cable between the fingers and examining the surface for the tiny cracks which indicate that perishing has begun. Alternatively a soft, swollen appearance of the insulation is characteristic of the deterioration caused by the action of oil or petrol.

When the time comes to renew the leads, don't be tempted to use ordinary rubber-covered or plastic-insulated high-tension cable. Later engines have suppressor-type high-tension leads which cut down radio and television interference (in addition to the special carbon brush in the distributor, mentioned earlier). These leads consist of an insulated covering, through the centre of which passes a rayon cord impregnated with carbon particles. At each end of the lead a short piece of copper wire passes into the centre of the cord and, at the sparking plug end, this is bent back so that it lies along the outside of the lead, thus providing an electrical contact between the rayon cord and the metal connector. A set of replacement leads, which can be obtained from a Ford dealer, should therefore be fitted. The leads are retained in the sockets of the coil and distributor simply by screwed sleeves.

Refitting the Distributor. If the pinch-bolt in the mounting plate has not been slackened, the original timing will be regained when the distributor is refitted to the engine. It is as well, however, to check the timing as described on page 75. Even a slight alteration in the contact-breaker gap will alter the timing by several degrees.

THE IGNITION COIL

The remaining component in the ignition system—if we exclude the ignition switch and the battery—is the ignition coil, which converts the low-voltage current from the battery into the high-tension current that is needed to produce a spark at the plug points.

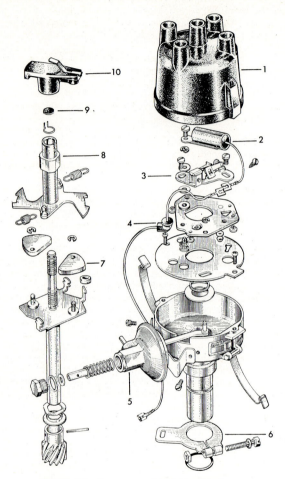

Fig. 37. The later type of ignition distributor

1. *Distributor cap*
2. *Condenser (capacitor)*
3. *Contact-breaker assembly*
4. *Low-tension feed wire*
5. *Vacuum timing control*
6. *Distributor clamp*
7. *Centrifugal timing weight*
8. *Cam*
9. *Felt lubricating washer*
10. *Rotor*

The ignition coil is a sealed, oil-insulated unit containing two windings: the primary—a relatively heavy winding consisting of a few hundred turns of wire which carry the battery current—and the secondary, which consists of many thousands of turns of fine wire, wound beneath the primary winding around an iron core. When the engine is running, current flows through the primary windings but is interrupted, at the instant at which each spark is required, by the opening of the contact points in the distributor which form, in effect, an automatic on-off switch driven by the engine.

This induces a very high current in the secondary winding—it may reach a peak of 30,000 volts—but in practice the voltage continues to rise only until it is sufficient to cause a spark to jump across the sparking plug gap. The voltage required depends on a number of factors, such as the compression pressure existing in the combustion chamber at that moment, the air-fuel ratio of the mixture, the sparking plug temperature and the width of the gap.

The coil is the one item in the ignition system that usually requires little or no attention, apart from keeping the external surface clean—particularly the moulded cap. Remember that a current which reaches a peak of many thousands of volts will always try to find a leakage path from the central terminal to one of the low-tension terminals or to the earthed metal case of the coil. Moisture or greasy dirt is very liable to form such a conducting path.

A coil may appear satisfactory when cold or for a short period after the engine has been started, but may develop a partial or complete open-circuit in the windings when it has become thoroughly warmed-up, causing misfiring or ignition failure. As the coil will resume its normal action as soon as it cools down, this can often prove a very elusive fault to diagnose. When special test equipment is not available the best plan is to substitute temporarily a coil that is known to be in good condition.

An interesting feature is the method used on later engines to provide a strong spark when starting from cold. The heavy current drain caused by the starter motor under these conditions reduces the battery voltage to as low as 9–10 volts instead of the nominal 12 volts, and this will seriously affect the efficiency of the ignition coil.

The solution is to use a low-voltage coil which can provide a good spark when supplied with this reduced battery voltage. When the starter switch is operated, the coil receives current through a wire which is connected to a terminal on the solenoid starter switch—not directly from the ignition switch. When the engine is running normally, however, the full battery voltage which is available would overload the coil. The current is there-fore fed through a resistor mounted on the coil, or through a special resistance feed wire, which connects the coil to the ignition switch and reduces the voltage to the correct figure.

One thus has the best of both worlds, but it is necessary to check that there are sound connections between the resistor and the coil terminal, or in the resistance wire between the coil and the ignition switch, as the case may be; there must also be a good connection between the coil and the terminal on the starter solenoid switch. Otherwise you can expect troubles such as difficult starting or misfiring.

IGNITION TIMING

A small alteration in the ignition timing—the instant at which the spark occurs in the combustion chamber—can have an appreciable effect on the performance and fuel consumption of the engine. Moreover the most effective timing at any moment depends on a number of factors which vary as running conditions change. The grade of fuel that is normally used also enters into the picture; "Premium" or "Super" fuels are less liable to detonate or pre-ignite than "regular" brands when the engine is pulling hard at low speeds, thus allowing a greater degree of ignition advance to be used than would otherwise be the case.

Before dealing with timing adjustments, therefore, the action of the automatic controls incorporated in the distributor must be briefly described. If these are not operating correctly the performance of the engine will be completely upset. Although the fact is seldom stressed in instruction books, the time spent on a thorough distributor check-over on one of the modern motor-driven test sets that are to be found in larger garages is seldom wasted.

Automatic Advance-retard Mechanism. Housed within the distributor body, beneath the contact-breaker baseplate, are two small bob-weights which are pivoted to a plate attached to the driving spindle so that they fly outwards, against the tension of retaining springs, as the engine speed rises. In doing so they rotate a sleeve that carries the cam, moving it further in the direction of rotation and thus advancing the ignition.

Provided that it receives regular lubrication, the centrifugal timing control seldom gives trouble. Sometimes a spring may break. If this happens, it is essential to renew both springs, making sure that they are of the correct part number for the engine, as their strength determines the shape of the advance curve. It is advisable to check the centrifugal control when the contact-breaker components have been dismantled for routine servicing as described earlier. It is necessary only to remove the screw that retains the cam on the shaft, pull off the cam, disconnect the vacuum control link from the peg on the upper moving plate of the assembly and remove the two screws that pass through lugs on the fixed plate, into the flange of the distributor body. Make a note of the positions of the various washers and terminal tags as they are removed and also of the relative positions of the slot in the cam that locates the rotor, and the offset driving dog at the base of the distributor shaft. It is possible to replace the cam 180° from the correct position.

When fitting new springs great care must be taken not to overstretch them or distort the spring eyes.

Vacuum Timing Control. The circular housing seen in Figs. 36 and 37 contains a diaphragm which responds to the variations that occur in the partial vacuum in the induction system between the carburettor and the cylinders. When the engine is running at a moderately high speed with the throttle partly closed—under main-road cruising conditions, for example—a relatively high vacuum exists and the diaphragm of the vacuum control unit rotates the contact-breaker baseplate in a clockwise direction against the direction of rotation of the cam, thus advancing the ignition timing. When the engine is pulling hard at low speeds with a wide throttle-opening on the other hand—conditions which call for a retarded ignition timing to prevent detonation and "pinking"—the vacuum in the induction system is low and the diaphragm is returned by spring pressure. The contact-breaker assembly then rotates anticlockwise and the ignition is retarded.

It will be seen that the action of the vacuum control either complements or opposes the action of the centrifugal control, ensuring that the most effective timing is maintained under all conditions of load and speed. A further point is that the suction connexion for the vacuum control is not made directly into the induction pipe but through a small drilling in the carburettor just on the atmospheric side of the throttle plate, so that the control is out of action when the throttle is closed and the engine is idling (when the vacuum in the induction system is high), thus preventing excessive ignition advance under these conditions.

Micrometer Timing Control. A further refinement on earlier distributors is that the static position of the contact-breaker baseplate can be varied over a small range of timing by rotating the knurled nut on the vacuum timing control, without disturbing the main setting of the distributor. Each of the divisions that registers with the edge of the housing represents a change in timing of 4 degrees at the crankshaft, so that the setting should not be altered more than, say, half a division at a time. It is worth remembering that one turn of the knurled adjusting knob is equivalent to three degrees of timing.

Obtaining the Correct Basic Setting. It is always best to have the ignition timing checked by a Ford dealer, who has special equipment which enables the setting to be determined quickly and accurately. But if this is not possible, the basic timing can be checked as follows—

Remove the sparking plugs, cover the sparking-plug hole nearest the radiator with your thumb and rotate the engine by means of the fan belt. You will be able to feel the suction and compression in the cylinder as the piston descends and then rises on the compression stroke. Watch the notch on the rim of the crankshaft pulley and slowly bring it into line with the pointer on the timing chain cover as the piston reaches the end of the compression stroke. An earlier in-line engine is now at top-dead-centre.

Twin timing pointers are provided on Cortina cross-flow engines and on

the Corsair V4 models. In the case of the Cortina, when the notch is
aligned with the left-hand pointer (the first to be reached as the engine
is rotated clockwise) the timing is set 10° B.T.D.C. The right-hand
pointer gives a setting of 6° B.T.D.C. If the notch is between the two
pointers, the setting is 8° B.T.D.C. On V4 engines, the first pointer to
be reached gives 8° B.T.D.C., and the second pointer, 4° B.T.D.C.

Fig. 38. Refitting the distributor

*The rotor must be in line with the terminal on the side of the body before the distributor is slid
home. The rotor will turn slightly as the gears mesh*

If the distributor has been removed from the engine, hold it so that the
vacuum control spindle is horizontal for in-line engines and with the vacuum
unit facing forward on V4 power units. On in-line engines turn the rotor
until it is aligned as shown in Fig. 38. On V4 engines, make sure that the
rotor is just before the position at which it will register with No. 1 contact
in the distributor cap. This is the right-hand rear electrode when the distributor is correctly fitted to the engine.

Slide the distributor into place. The rotor will turn clockwise slightly,
towards the condenser, as the driving gears engage.

Fit the setscrew and lockwasher that secure the clamp beneath the
distributor to the cylinder block and slacken the clamping bolt in the split
clamp so that the distributor body can be rotated. Set the micrometer
adjustment so that the fourth graduation on the scale is just showing.

Now rotate the distributor clockwise to take up any backlash in the
drive, keeping a light finger pressure on the rotor, also in a clockwise

direction, until the contact-breaker points are just about to separate. The spark will now take place at top-dead-centre. When the distributor is fitted with a knurled timing adjustment nut (shown at 5 in Fig. 34), it is an easy matter to provide the correct amount of ignition advance, as specified in Chapter 1, by turning the adjusting nut in the direction of A, as shown by the arrow on the housing. Each division on the vernier scale represents an alteration in timing of four degrees. To set the timing 6° advanced, therefore, the scale will have to be moved to the extent of 1½ divisions.

Later distributors do not have this convenient adjusting nut and it is therefore necessary to slacken the distributor clamping bolt and to rotate the distributor body in order to obtain the correct setting. Tighten the bolt securely after making the adjustment, but do not over-tighten it as this will distort the clamp.

Two practical tips: *Never set the timing after rotating the engine backwards*; the backlash in the timing chain can cause an appreciable error. Secondly, it is difficult to assess the exact moment at which the contact points separate but if the ignition is switched on, it is usually possible to see and hear a small spark which occurs as contact is broken. A more accurate method of timing is to connect a twelve-volt sidelamp or warning-lamp bulb, mounted in a suitable holder, between the low-tension terminal on the side of the distributor body and an earthed point on the engine. At the instant that the contacts separate the lamp will light up. After adjusting the timing, rotate the engine through several revolutions and then recheck the setting.

Don't forget to reconnect the vacuum-advance pipe to the distributor body when the timing is correct. If the distributor has not been removed, it is better to disconnect this pipe before altering the timing, and then to bend it gently so that it fits the union on the distributor without strain. Be careful not to kink the pipe, however.

Checking the Timing on the Road. The static setting should be regarded only as the starting point for a series of road tests during which the timing can be precisely adjusted by the micrometer control on the distributor, to suit the condition of the engine and the fuel that will normally be used. It is often recommended that the timing should be progressively advanced until the engine just shows signs of pinking under full throttle on a moderately steep hill. While this method gives quite good results with less highly tuned engines which will run on "regular" and "mixture" fuels, however, some premium fuels have such high anti-knock values that the possibility of over-advancing the engine before pinking occurs cannot be ruled out.

The method favoured by tuning enthusiasts is to make a series of tests on a level road, noting carefully, by stop-watch readings, the time taken to accelerate from 20 m.p.h. to 50 m.p.h. in top gear, with the throttle fully open in each case and over the same stretch of road, so that each test is conducted under precisely similar conditions. The best ignition setting is that which results in the shortest time to accelerate over the speed range. This will also give the most economical fuel consumption.

Alternatively, start each test from a given point and note the point at which the higher speed is reached, by reference to bushes by the roadside, fencing posts or similar identifying marks.

When altering the timing by the roadside, turn the micrometer adjuster only three or four clicks at a time or rotate the distributor through only a fraction of an inch, as this adjustment is very sensitive. If in doubt concerning the ignition timing, have it checked by a Ford dealer who has a stroboscopic timing light which enables the behaviour of the centrifugal and vacuum controls to be observed under actual running conditions.

8 The electrical equipment and instruments

ARE you one of those owners who will cheerfully tackle any mechanical jobs but tend to fight shy of anything to do with the "electrics?" If so, you can take heart: no specialized knowledge of electricity is needed to service the electrical equipment—at any rate as far as normal routine maintenance is concerned. When a fault develops which is beyond simple first-aid measures, of course (such as tightening a loose connexion or renewing or insulating a broken or chafed lead), it is always advisable to enlist the aid of a specialist. The service-exchange scheme operated by Ford dealers and Lucas service depots, under which a faulty component is replaced by a reconditioned, guaranteed unit at a fixed charge, is well worth investigating when trouble does crop up.

On later models the *negative* terminal of the battery is earthed, conforming with the policy which aims at bringing British vehicles into line with the practice adopted by the rest of the world.

Special care must therefore be taken when ordering and installing replacement equipment. In particular, a transistor radio will be seriously damaged if it is connected so that its polarity is reversed. Dynamos, control units and similar replacements can also be supplied, polarized for either positive or negative earth, so trouble should not be experienced if the difference in polarity is borne in mind.

THE BATTERY

We can begin our survey of the electrical system logically with the battery, which stores up, by an electro-chemical process, the electrical energy provided by the dynamo (or by an external battery charger) and feeds it as required to the ignition, lighting, starting and accessory circuits. The battery is therefore the heart of the system, providing a reserve of current when the dynamo is not charging. But it must be admitted that in the compact type of battery fitted to most modern cars, this reserve is rather limited. In fact a fully-charged battery can become almost completely discharged during the course of a long winter evening and night if the car is left parked with the side, tail, number-plate and panel lights switched on.

Yet battery troubles are largely avoidable. There is no reason why the life of a first-class battery should not be extended to at least four years,

by following the advice given in this chapter. These jobs are additional
to the routine topping-up of the cells described in Chapter 4, by the way.
If some of the information that follows seems a little technical, at least it
has the merit of saving money in the long run!

Battery Service. The filler plugs should be kept clean and tight to prevent acid leakage, and the battery and the surrounding parts—particularly
the tops of the cells—must be clean and dry, to prevent corrosion and
leakage of current. The cells will require topping-up with distilled water
from time to time, as also described in Chapter IV.

Occasionally, the connectors should be removed so that the contact
surfaces can be examined and any corrosion scraped off. Before they are
refitted they should be lightly smeared with petroleum jelly. Gently tap
the connectors on to the terminal posts with the wooden handle of a
screwdriver and do not overtighten the retaining screws, or they may
strip the threads in the lead terminal posts. Similarly, the battery-retaining
clamp should be just sufficiently tight to prevent movement of the battery
on its mounting but not so tight that it cracks or distorts the battery case.

Idle Batteries. A battery which is not likely to be used for some time
should be charged at the normal charging rate of $4-4\frac{1}{2}$ amperes until the
specific gravity is within 0·010 of the fully-charged value or until the cells
are "gassing." The leads should be disconnected to avoid loss of charge
through any small leak in the wiring. The battery can then be kept in
condition for immediate use by giving it a freshening charge at least once
every two months. It should, preferably, also be given a thorough charge
after an idle period, before it is put into service. It is unwise to allow a
battery that is in good condition to stand for more than two months
without charging it. It would be better to leave it with the local garage
or electrical service station.

Charging the Battery. The charging rate of the dynamo or generator,
which is of the two-brush compensated voltage-current control type, is
automatically regulated. It depends on three factors: the state of charge
of the battery, the prevailing atmospheric temperature and the current
that is being drawn by the various circuits at any given moment. Thus the
regulator provides a large charging current when the battery is discharged,
the rate being highest in cold weather; as the battery becomes charged
the charging rate is reduced, tapering off to a "trickle" charge that keeps
a fully-charged battery in good condition.

To prevent the battery discharging through the generator circuit whenever the engine is stopped or is running at low speeds, an electro-magnetic
switch—the cut-out—is combined with the regulator in the control box.
When the cut-out points open, and if the ignition is switched on, a red
warning light glows in the ignition and lighting switch panel. Although
this is usually termed the ignition warning light—as one of its functions
is to remind you not to leave the ignition switched on when the engine is
not running—it will be seen that it also serves as a warning that the

dynamo is not charging, if it fails to go out whenever the engine is speeded up above idling speed. If the light glows at normal running speeds, therefore, first check that the fan belt is intact and correctly tensioned; then have the dynamo and regulator checked over by an electrical specialist.

The ammeter, when fitted, supplements the ignition warning light. It indicates the balance between the charge being supplied by the dynamo and the rate at which current is being drawn from the battery. Immediately after a cold start the needle should move fairly well across towards the +30 mark, since, as already explained, the regulator is designed to give the battery a "boosting" charge to compensate for the heavy current drawn by the starter motor. Within a few miles, however, the needle should drop back approximately to the central position, showing that the battery is receiving only a trickle charge. When the headlights or electrically-operated accessories are switched on, the ammeter may temporarily show a discharge but the regulator should quickly come into action and restore the balance. If a continuous discharge reading is shown, do not be tempted to overlook the warning in the hope that matters will put themselves right. The battery can become discharged in a surprisingly short time, and you may find yourself stranded when next you try to start the engine. Have a check made by a qualified auto-electrician at the earliest possible opportunity.

It is also best to obtain expert advice if it is thought that the charging rate is too high. A high rate will be indicated by the need for very frequent topping-up of the cells as the result of excessive "gassing" of the electrolyte. When adjusting the regulator, accurate voltage and amperage readings must be taken with high-grade moving-coil meters. This rules out any makeshift methods of adjustment—which applies not only to the owner but also to a garage which does not have the necessary equipment!

Home Charging. Many owners look on a home charger primarily as an insurance against occasional battery exhaustion, rather than as a useful aid to battery maintenance. But the relatively short life obtained from many modern batteries can often be ascribed to the heavy "boost" charge of up to 20–25 amperes which they receive when a car is driven away after a cold start. The correct normal charging rate for the battery is $4-4\frac{1}{2}$ amperes.

Obviously, if a home charger is installed and the battery is kept at or near the fully-charged condition, it will have a much easier life and the cost of the charger will eventually be more than saved; moreover, one has on the credit side the peace of mind that results from the certainty of an immediate start even on the coldest mornings. A very useful accessory —particularly to those such as doctors who must be able to depend on an instant start—is a time switch to control the charger; Sangamo Weston Ltd., of Enfield, Middlesex, make an excellent range. Most owners would probably choose a switch that can be set to omit any day of the week on which the car is not used.

THE DYNAMO OR GENERATOR

The routine maintenance needed by the dynamo is confined to checking the tension of the driving belt every 6,000 miles as described in Chapter IV and lubricating the rear bearing at 18,000-mile intervals by applying a few drops of engine oil to the hole in the bearing housing. Specialist attention (also, say, at 18,000-mile intervals) entails inspection and cleaning of the commutator and brushes; it is preferable to leave this to a Ford dealer who will, at the same time, be able to check and if necessary adjust the charging regulator. If the work is done at home, however, the dynamo should be removed and the long bolts that retain the end-plate at the opposite end to the pulley should be extracted. With the plate removed, the commutator (the assembly of copper segments at the end of the rotating armature) and the brushes can be examined.

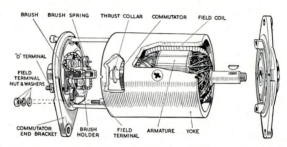

Fig. 39. Dynamo partly dismantled for attention to the brushes and commutator

Clean the commutator. If it is scored, it should be taken to an electrical specialist, who will skim it in a lathe. Check that the brushes move freely in their holders. If they stick, clean them and their holders with a petrol-moistened cloth.

If the brushes have worn down to a minimum length of about $\frac{3}{8}$ in., renew them. If worn but serviceable brushes are refitted, make sure that they are inserted in their original positions, to maintain the correct "bedding" on the commutator.

When reassembling the end-plate, trap the brushes in the raised position by side pressure from their springs and finally release and position the springs by passing a screwdriver through the inspection holes in the plate, when the latter is fully home.

THE STARTER MOTOR AND SWITCH

Probably the most important of the auxiliaries that draw current from the battery is the starter motor. Unlike the generator, it is in action only intermittently and therefore normally has a long, trouble-free life; because it requires no periodic lubrication it is, in fact, often overlooked by the average owner. The starter should be serviced, however, at reasonable intervals—say, every 18,000 miles—when it should be removed from the car and dismantled by an expert, as in the case of the dynamo, so that the commutator, brushes and the drive components can be inspected and cleaned.

As the starter has a detachable cover-band over the brushes and commutator, these items can be inspected without the need for removing the end plate (as is necessary with the generator). Otherwise the servicing is similar to that previously described. Brushes which have worn down to a length of $\frac{5}{16}$ in. should be renewed.

Testing the Starter. Assuming that the battery is in a charged condition, switch on the lights and press the starter switch. If the lights go dim, although the starter does not operate, either the battery is discharged or current is flowing through the windings of the starter but for some reason the armature is not rotating, possibly because the starter pinion is already engaged with the flywheel starter-ring.

If the lamps remain bright, however, the starter switch may be faulty. A more likely trouble, nevertheless, is loose or corroded connexions on the ignition switch or on the solenoid-operated switch. The latter, which is mounted in the engine compartment close to the battery, can be tested by pressing on the rubber dust cover. If the starter then operates, but does not do so when the ignition switch is turned fully clockwise, the trouble must obviously lie in the ignition switch, in the solenoid or in the wiring between the two.

The under-bonnet switch is a convenient method of starting the engine when making adjustments. The ignition must, of course, be switched on and a special check should be made to ensure that the gear lever is in neutral.

Freeing a Jammed Starter Pinion. If the starter pinion should become jammed in mesh with the starter ring it can usually be freed by engaging top gear and attempting to rock the car forwards. It is a common mistake to engage a lower gear and rock the car violently backwards and forwards; this usually jams the pinion more firmly in mesh and may damage the drive.

If rocking the car forwards does not free the pinion, the squared extension of the spindle should be rotated in a clockwise direction with a spanner. Admittedly this is rather inaccessible and if a dust cap is fitted, this must be prised off.

If Starter Does Not Engage. If the starter pinion does not engage with the flywheel and the motor whirrs idly, the starter drive probably requires cleaning. It will be necessary to unbolt the starter from the engine, supporting it from below (it is surprisingly heavy). The pinion should move freely on the screwed sleeve; any dirt must be washed off with paraffin. A trace of paraffin should then be applied to the sleeve; oil must not be used owing to the risk of grit accumulating and causing the pinion to stick.

If the battery is discharged or weak, the starter may spin once or twice without engaging. This is a useful warning of the trouble that can occur in the future, when you may be stranded until a new battery or a tow is obtained.

Starting in Winter. In very cold weather it may be an advantage to depress the clutch pedal to relieve the starter of the drag of the cold, thick oil in the transmission. On the other hand, the friction of the clutch release bearing may be sufficient to slow down the cranking speed. Make a test under both conditions. Operate the starter switch firmly and release it immediately the engine fires.

HEADLAMPS

As a general rule, the headlamps should be adjusted so that when the main beam filaments are alight, the beams are pointing straight ahead, parallel both to each other and to the ground. This will automatically give the correct position for the dipped beams. Allowance must be made, of course, for special conditions. For example, if the rear of the car is heavily loaded it will be necessary to lower the main beams slightly to avoid any risk of oncoming traffic being dazzled when the beams are in the dipped position. It will also be necessary to comply with any local regulations that may be in force. Remember, too, that as the bulbs age, the prefocused filaments may sag and upset the focus and direction of the beams.

Renewing the Light Units. It is unnecessary to disturb the setting of the adjusting screws when removing the combined bulb and reflector units (Fig. 40). The inner lamps have single filaments and the outer lamps double. Should a filament fail, it is necessary to renew the unit. The connector is simply a push fit on pins projecting from the rear of the light unit.

Removal and replacement of the unit will not affect the alignment of the lamp beams but these can be set, if necessary, by rotating the two trimmer screws that position the seating rim behind the light unit. These should be screwed in as far as possible and then unscrewed a little at a time until the correct alignment is obtained. The top screw controls the beam in a vertical plane, the side screw aims it in a horizontal plane. Ford dealers, incidentally, have special equipment that enables the alignment to be correctly set in a matter of minutes.

ELECTRICAL ACCESSORIES

Windscreen Wiper. The electrically-operated wiper normally requires no attention, other than renewal of the wiper blades at least once a year. Even blades that are in good condition cannot be effective, however, if the glass has acquired a coating of "traffic film," consisting largely of deposits caused by exhaust fumes (diesel-engined vehicles are particularly bad offenders in this respect) which result in persistent smearing of the raindrops in the path of the wiper blades. The silicones used in many modern car polishes can create a similar effect.

In either case the most satisfactory remedy is to clean the screen thoroughly with a liquid detergent, used undiluted. This should be of a non-bleaching type; the preparations sold for domestic washing-up purposes are excellent. Strong detergents may discolour the paintwork if

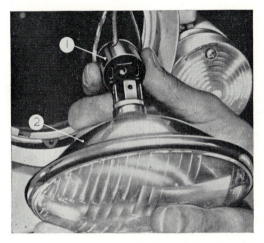

Fig. 40. Fitting a new headlamp light unit
1. Push-on connector. 2. Combined bulb and reflector unit

allowed to remain on it for any length of time. In no circumstances should any abrasives be used as the glass is easily scratched. For the same reason, the wiper blades should not be kept in action on a dry screen.

If the blades do not sweep through satisfactory arcs, or fail to park neatly when the wiper is switched off (they are self-parking), it is possible that at some time the arms have been incorrectly fitted to the driving spindles. No attempt should be made to rotate the arms while they are still attached to their spindles, as they engage with finely-cut splines that allow them to be accurately and positively positioned. Each arm must therefore be withdrawn by lifting a small retaining clip with the tip of a screwdriver and then refitting it in the desired position.

Electric Horns. An adjustment is provided on the fixed contact of each horn but this is intended only to compensate for wear on the moving parts that takes place over a long period of use; it does not alter the note and should not normally be disturbed, as an ammeter should be used when making any adjustment. The maximum current drawn by each horn should not exceed 6 amperes for the Clear Hooter horn and 6–7 amperes for the Lucas type.

When a horn fails to sound or becomes erratic in action, however, the trouble can most usually be traced to a loose or dirty contact, to a break in the wiring or to a faulty horn relay (when fitted). An apparent change in the note, on the other hand, is usually caused either by loose mounting bolts (although the horn itself is flexibly mounted, the mounting bolts must be kept tight) or by sympathetic vibration of some component in the vicinity of the horn.

Flashing Indicators. The flashing indicator lamps are fed with inter-mittent current from a sealed control unit. This contains a switch which is actuated by the alternate expansion and contraction of a length of wire that is heated by the current passing to the indicator lamps, thus giving a flashing frequency of about 80–100 times per minute.

Failure or erratic action of the flashing indicators may be caused by dirty contacts in the indicator switch, in the wiring, or by a "blown" fuse (*see* page 87). If the fuse is in order, the flasher unit is probably faulty. It is not repairable. If the indicator lamps light up when the B and L terminals on the unit are connected together and the direction indicator switch is operated with the ignition switched on, the unit must be replaced. The new unit should be handled with care as it is a somewhat delicate component and can be put out of action if it is dropped or receives a moderately hard knock.

Fuel Gauge. It is normal for the pointer to take several seconds to register the correct reading after the ignition has been switched on. It is deflected by a bimetal strip which bends as current passes through a heating coil wound around it. A small voltage regulator supplies the current at 7–10 volts and also feeds the temperature indicator, when this is fitted. The transmitter fitted to the petrol tank contains a resistance which is varied by the movements of the float as the petrol level rises or falls.

Fault-tracing with this type of gauge is confined to making sure that current is reaching the voltage regulator and that this is supplying the correct voltage. If necessary, fit a replacement regulator, making sure that the B and E terminals are uppermost and are not more than 20 degrees from the vertical. If the gauge still does not operate correctly when the ignition is switched on, there is little than can be done except to check for the continuity of the wiring between the gauge and the tank unit and then to substitute a serviceable unit for each in turn.

Temperature Gauge. The temperature gauge operates on a similar principle to the fuel gauge, except that the "transmitter" is a bulb in the thermostat housing at the front of the engine which contains a pellet of material, the electrical resistance of which varies with changes in temperature. Should the gauge give trouble, check that current at the correct voltage is reaching the instrument from the voltage regulator and that the wire between the gauge and the resistance element is sound, with clean, secure connexions. If either the gauge or the temperature element is faulty a new unit must be fitted. When making tests, never connect either unit individually to the battery.

WIRING AND FUSES

When it is necessary to carry out systematic fault-tracing, or when the time comes to renew all or part of the wiring, a detailed wiring diagram is, of course, invaluable. Fault-tracing then becomes a matter of starting from the appropriate source of current and working progressively through the circuit until the fault is discovered. In this respect the detailed Ford wiring diagrams, as exemplified by Figs. 41–50, in this chapter are particularly clear and useful.

Remember that current that reaches a lamp or accessory must eventually return to the battery through the metal of the car. The vital importance of sound "earth" connexions is often overlooked. Metal-to-metal joints must be scraped clean and bright and the securing screws or nuts must be firmly tightened.

Connecting-up Accessories. Normally, connexions should be made to one of the two terminals marked *B* in the current-voltage control box. Remember that the additional items are not controlled by the ignition switch. so there is a risk of discharging the battery should they be inadvertently switched on when the engine is not running. On the other hand, if it is desired to use a radio when the engine is switched off, connect it to the terminal on the ignition switch shown in the wiring diagram. It will then be brought into action (without switching on the ignition) when the key is turned to the left.

Fuses. On early cars the direction indicator flasher unit, and the heater and radio (when these are fitted), are protected by individual 5-amp fuses which are held in plastic carriers inserted in the wires feeding the components, behind the instrument panel. The flasher unit fuse is inserted in a green-coloured feed wire, the heater fuse in a white wire and the radio fuse in a blue-brown wire.

The holders have a bayonet locking action. On the majority of later cars the only fuse provided is that in the lead which supplies the radio, but the Cortina 1300 and 1600 are exceptions, having a fuse box mounted on the engine bulkhead which contains six fuses, protecting the side and tail lamps and the headlamp dip beam and main beam, the circuits

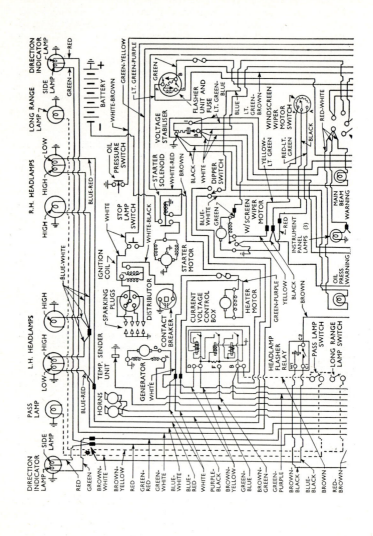

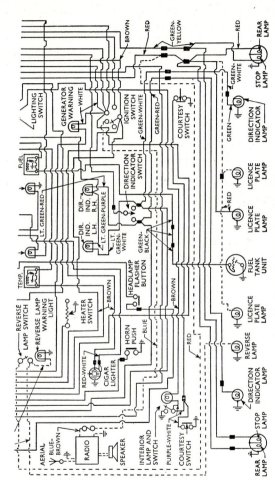

Fig. 41. Typical wiring diagram, Classic

Optional accessory circuits are shown by dotted lines, except for rear licence plate lamps required by certain overseas territories. Wire marked * from headlamp relay flasher terminal C1 is connected to main or low-beam connector, depending on requirements. When flasher is not permitted, relay is not required and connecting wires are taped-up in main wiring assembly being divided between the two sides of the car. The fuses are identified on the cover of the fuse box.

Always replace a burnt-out fuse with one of the correct value. If the new fuse blows immediately, check over the wiring from the fuse to the item that it protects. If you cannot see any obvious signs of short-circuiting, have the component tested by a specialist.

If the correct replacement fuse cannot be obtained at short notice, a makeshift repair can be carried out by clipping the ends of a short length of 5-amp household fuse wire between the caps of the burnt-out fuse and the contacts in each half of the holder. Another get-you-home dodge is to bridge the fuse in a similar way with a strip of silver foil from a cigarette packet.

Rewiring the Car. Rewiring the car is a major operation, not to be tackled lightly by the novice. To have the work carried out professionally, however, is apt to be somewhat expensive and it is not surprising that many practically-minded owners decide to undertake the work themselves. By far the simplest—and in the long run, usually the cheapest—method of tackling the job is to obtain a complete wiring "harness" from a specialist firm, such as Autosparks Ltd. of Lime Street, Hull. All that is necessary is to remove the existing wiring a section at a time, replacing it with the new harness. It is virtually impossible to go wrong if each step is checked.

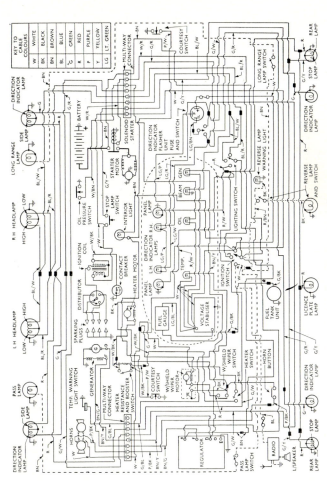

Fig. 42. Wiring diagram for earlier Cortina

4

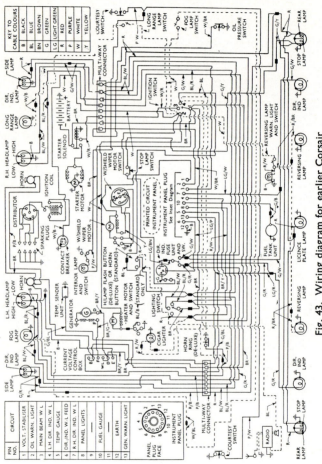

Fig. 43. Wiring diagram for earlier Corsair

KEY TO CABLE COLOURS	
B	BLACK
BL	BLUE
BN	BROWN
G	GREEN
LG	LIGHT GREEN
P	PURPLE
R	RED
W	WHITE
Y	YELLOW

PIN NO.	CIRCUIT
1	VOLT. STABILISER
2	OIL WARN. LIGHT
3	MAIN BEAM W.L
4	L.H. DIR. IND. W.L
5	TEMP GAUGE
6	DIR. IND. W.L FEED
7	R.H. DIR. IND. W.L
8	PANEL LIGHTS
9	
10	FUEL GAUGE
11	
12	EARTH
13	GEN. WARN. LIGHT

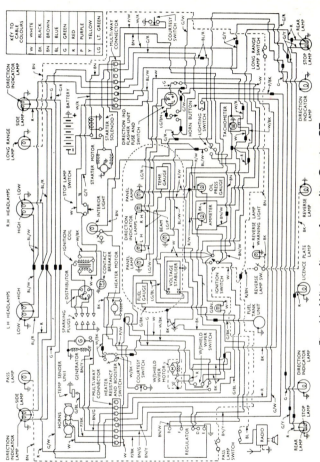

Fig. 44. Wiring diagram for earlier Cortina GT

KEY TO CABLE COLOURS	
W	WHITE
BK	BLACK
BN	BROWN
BL	BLUE
G	GREEN
P	PURPLE
R	RED
Y	YELLOW
LG	LT. GREEN

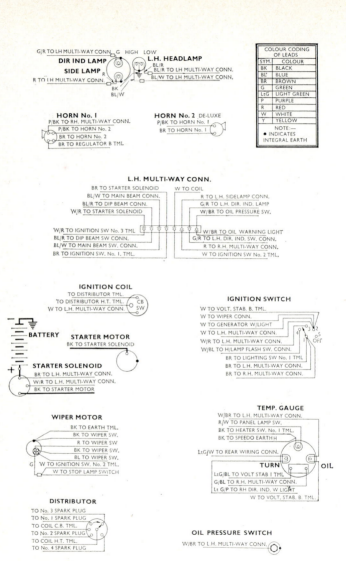

G/R TO LH MULTI-WAY CONN. G HIGH LOW
DIR IND LAMP **L.H. HEADLAMP**
SIDE LAMP R
R TO LH MULTI-WAY CONN.
BL/R
BL/R TO LH MULTI-WAY CONN.
BL/W TO LH MULTI-WAY CONN.
BK
BL/W

COLOUR CODING OF LEADS	
SYM.	COLOUR
BK	BLACK
BL'	BLUE
BR	BROWN
G	GREEN
LtG	LIGHT GREEN
P	PURPLE
R	RED
W	WHITE
Y	YELLOW

NOTE:—
● INDICATES
INTEGRAL EARTH

HORN No. I
P/BK TO RH. MULTI-WAY CONN.
P/BK TO HORN No. 2
BR TO HORN No. 2
BR TO REGULATOR B TML.

HORN No. 2 DE-LUXE
P/BK TO HORN No. I
BR TO HORN No. I

L.H. MULTI-WAY CONN.
BR TO STARTER SOLENOID   W TO COIL
BL/W TO MAIN BEAM CONN.   R TO L.H. SIDELAMP CONN.
BL/R TO DIP BEAM CONN.   G/R TO L.H. DIR. IND. LAMP
W/R TO STARTER SOLENOID   W/BR TO OIL PRESSURE SW.
W/R TO IGNITION SW No. 3 TML.   W/BR TO OIL WARNING LIGHT
BL/R TO DIP BEAM SW CONN.   G/R TO L.H. DIR. IND. SW. CONN.
BL/W TO MAIN BEAM SW. CONN.   R TO R.H. MULTI-WAY CONN.
BR TO IGNITION SW. No. I TML.   W TO IGNITION SW No. 2 TML.

IGNITION COIL
TO DISTRIBUTOR TML.
TO DISTRIBUTOR H.T. TML.   CB
W TO L.H. MULTI-WAY CONN.   SW

BATTERY
STARTER MOTOR
BK TO STARTER SOLENOID

STARTER SOLENOID
BR TO L.H. MULTI-WAY CONN.
W/R TO L.H. MULTI-WAY CONN.
BK TO STARTER MOTOR

IGNITION SWITCH
W TO VOLT. STAB. B. TML.
W TO WIPER CONN.
W TO GENERATOR W/LIGHT
W TO L.H. MULTI-WAY CONN.
W/R TO L.H. MULTI-WAY CONN.
W/BL TO H/LAMP FLASH SW. CONN.
BR TO LIGHTING SW No. I TML
BR TO L.H. MULTI-WAY CONN.
BR TO R.H. MULTI-WAY CONN.

WIPER MOTOR
BK TO EARTH TML.
BK TO WIPER SW.
R TO WIPER SW
BK TO WIPER SW.
BL TO WIPER SW.
G W TO IGNITION SW. No. 2 CONN.
W TO STOP LAMP SWITCH

TEMP. GAUGE
W/BR TO L.H. MULTI-WAY CONN.
R/W TO PANEL LAMP SW.
BK TO HEATER SW. No. I TML.
BK TO SPEEDO EARTH H
LtG/W TO REAR WIRING CONN.
TURN   OIL
LtG/BL TO VOLT STAB I TML
G/BL TO R.H. MULTI-WAY CONN.
Lt G/P TO RH DIR. IND. W LIGHT
W TO VOLT. STAB. B. TML.

DISTRIBUTOR
TO No. 3 SPARK PLUG
TO No. I SPARK PLUG
TO COIL C.B. TML.
TO No. 2 SPARK PLUG
TO COIL H.T. TML.
TO No. 4 SPARK PLUG

OIL PRESSURE SWITCH
W/BR TO L.H. MULTI-WAY CONN.

Fig. 45. Wiring diagram for Corsair V4

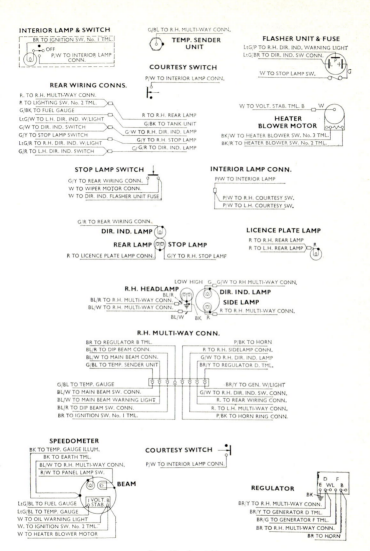

INTERIOR LAMP & SWITCH
BR TO IGNITION SW. No. I TML.
OFF
P/W TO INTERIOR LAMP CONN.

G/BL TO R.H. MULTI-WAY CONN.
TEMP. SENDER UNIT

FLASHER UNIT & FUSE
LtG/P TO R.H. DIR. IND. WARNING LIGHT
LtG/BR TO DIR. IND. SW CONN.
W TO STOP LAMP SW.

COURTESY SWITCH
P/W TO INTERIOR LAMP CONN.

REAR WIRING CONNS.
R. TO R.H. MULTI-WAY CONN.
R TO LIGHTING SW. No. 2 TML.
G/BK TO FUEL GAUGE
LtG/W TO L.H. DIR. IND. W/LIGHT
G/W TO DIR. IND. SWITCH
G/Y TO STOP LAMP SWITCH
LtG/R TO R.H. DIR. IND. W/LIGHT
G/R TO L.H. DIR. IND. SWITCH

R TO R.H. REAR LAMP
G/BK TO TANK UNIT
G/W TO R.H. DIR. IND. LAMP
G/Y TO R.H. STOP LAMP
G/GR TO DIR. IND. LAMP

W TO VOLT. STAB. TML. B   W
HEATER BLOWER MOTOR
BK/W TO HEATER BLOWER SW. No. 3 TML.
BK/R TO HEATER BLOWER SW. No. 2 TML.

STOP LAMP SWITCH
G/Y TO REAR WIRING CONN.
W TO WIPER MOTOR CONN.
W TO DIR. IND. FLASHER UNIT FUSE

INTERIOR LAMP CONN.
P/W TO INTERIOR LAMP
P/W TO R.H. COURTESY SW.
P/W TO L.H. COURTESY SW.

G/R TO REAR WIRING CONN.
DIR. IND. LAMP
REAR LAMP **STOP LAMP**
R TO LICENCE PLATE LAMP CONN.   G/Y TO R.H. STOP LAMP

LICENCE PLATE LAMP
R TO R.H. REAR LAMP
R TO L.H. REAR LAMP

LOW HIGH G G/W TO RH MULTI-WAY CONN.
R.H. HEADLAMP
BL/R
BL/R TO R.H. MULTI-WAY CONN.
BL/W TO R.H. MULTI-WAY CONN.
BL/W   BK R
DIR. IND. LAMP
SIDE LAMP
R TO R.H. MULTI-WAY CONN.

R.H. MULTI-WAY CONN.
BR TO REGULATOR B TML.
BL/R TO DIP BEAM CONN.
BL/W TO MAIN BEAM CONN.
G/BL TO TEMP. SENDER UNIT

P/BK TO HORN
R TO R.H. SIDELAMP CONN.
G/W TO R.H. DIR. IND. LAMP
BR/Y TO REGULATOR D. TML.

G/BL TO TEMP. GAUGE
BL/W TO MAIN BEAM SW. CONN.
BL/W TO MAIN BEAM WARNING LIGHT
BL/R TO DIP BEAM SW. CONN.
BR TO IGNITION SW. No. I TML.

BR/Y TO GEN. W/LIGHT
G/W TO R.H. DIR. IND. SW. CONN.
R. TO REAR WIRING CONN.
R. TO L.H. MULTI-WAY CONN.
P/BK TO HORN RING CONN.

SPEEDOMETER
BK TO TEMP. GAUGE ILLUM.
BK TO EARTH TML.
BL/W TO R.H. MULTI-WAY CONN.
R/W TO PANEL LAMP SW.
BEAM
I VOLT. B STAB.
LtG/BL TO FUEL GAUGE
LtG/BL TO TEMP. GAUGE
W TO OIL WARNING LIGHT
W. TO IGNITION SW. No. 2 TML.
W TO HEATER BLOWER MOTOR

COURTESY SWITCH
P/W TO INTERIOR LAMP CONN.

REGULATOR
D F
E WL B
BK
BR/Y TO R.H. MULTI-WAY CONN.
BR/Y TO GENERATOR D TML.
BR/G TO GENERATOR F TML.
BR TO R.H. MULTI-WAY CONN.
BR TO HORN

Fig. 45. (*contd.*)

95

LIGHTING SWITCH
BR. TO INTERIOR LAMP
BR TO IGNITION SW. No.1 TML.
R TO PANEL LAMP SWITCH
R TO REAR WIRING CONNECTION
BL TO H LAMP DIP SWITCH CONN.

CIGAR LIGHTER CONN.
R/W TO PANEL LAMP SW.
R/W TO FUEL GAUGE ILLUM.

EARTH TML.
STEERING COLUMN BRACE
BK TO SPEEDO EARTH
BK TO FUEL GAUGE ILLUM.
BK TO WIPER MOTOR

G/W TO REAR WIRING CONN.
DIR. IND. LAMP
STOP LAMP   **REAR LAMP**
G/Y TO REAR WIRING CONN.   R TO REAR WIRING CONN.
G/Y TO L.H. STOP LAMP   R TO LICENCE PLATE LAMP CONN.

WIPER MOTOR SWITCH

PANEL LAMP SWITCH
R TO LIGHTING SW. No. 2 TML.
R/W TO CIGAR LIGHTER CONN.
R/W TO SPEEDO ILLUM. LAMP
R/W TO TEMP. GAUGE ILLUM.

BK TO WIPER MOTOR
R TO WIPER MOTOR
BK TO WIPER MOTOR
BL TO WIPER MOTOR

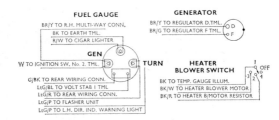

FUEL GAUGE
BR/Y TO R.H. MULTI-WAY CONN.
BK TO EARTH TML.
R/W TO CIGAR LIGHTER

GENERATOR
BR/Y TO REGULATOR D.TML.
BR/G TO REGULATOR F TML.

GEN   **TURN**
W TO IGNITION SW. No. 2 TML.
G/BK TO REAR WIRING CONN.
LtG/BL TO VOLT STAB 1 TML
LtG/R TO REAR WIRING CONN.
LtG/P TO FLASHER UNIT
LtG/P TO L.H. DIR. IND. WARNING LIGHT

HEATER BLOWER SWITCH
BK TO TEMP. GAUGE ILLUM.
BK/W TO HEATER BLOWER MOTOR
BK/R TO HEATER B/MOTOR RESISTOR

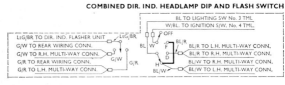

COMBINED DIR. IND. HEADLAMP DIP AND FLASH SWITCH
BL TO LIGHTING SW No. 3 TML.
W/BL. TO IGNITION S/W. No. 4 TML.
LtG/BR TO DIR. IND. FLASHER UNIT
G/W TO REAR WIRING CONN.
G/W TO R.H. MULTI-WAY CONN.
G/R TO REAR WIRING CONN.
G/R TO L.H. MULTI-WAY CONN.
BL/R TO L.H. MULTI-WAY CONN.
BL/R TO R.H. MULTI-WAY CONN.
BL/W TO R.H. MULTI-WAY CONN.
BL/W TO L.H. MULTI-WAY CONN.

FUEL TANK UNIT
G/BK TO REAR WIRING CONN.

P/BK TO RH. MULTI-WAY CONN.   P/BK
HORN RING

Fig. 45. (*contd.*)

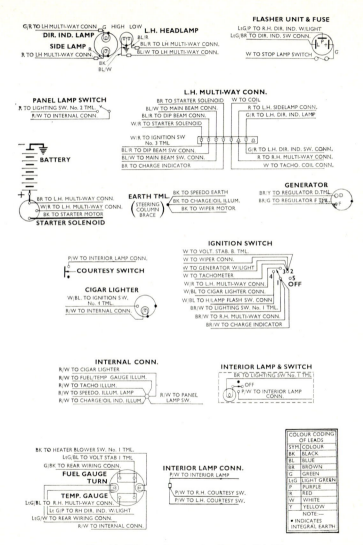

Fig. 46. Wiring diagram for Corsair V4 GT

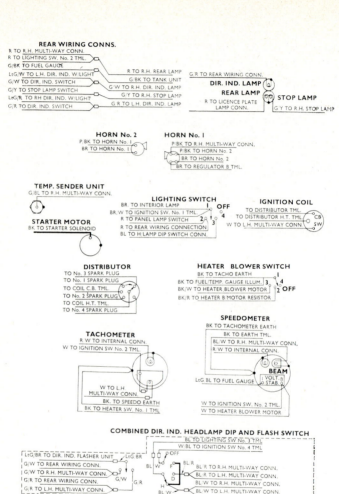

Fig. 46. (contd.)

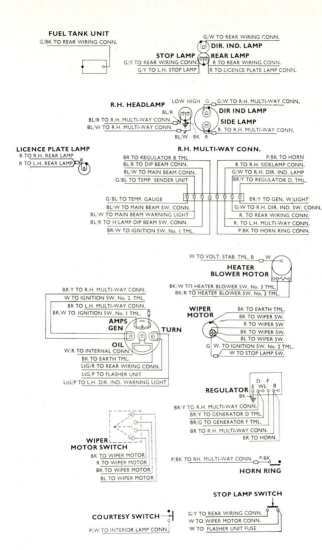

Fig. 46. (contd.)

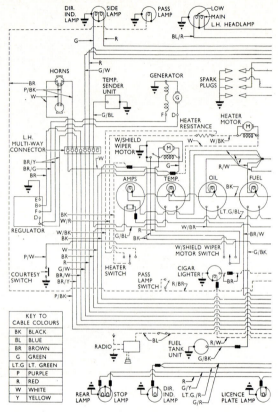

Fig. 47. Wiring diagram for Cortina GT

KEY TO CABLE COLOURS	
BK	BLACK
BL	BLUE
BR	BROWN
G	GREEN
LT.G	LT. GREEN
P	PURPLE
R	RED
W	WHITE
Y	YELLOW

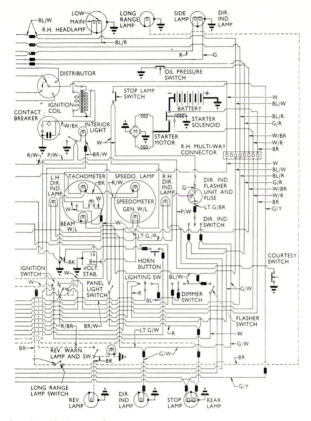

October 1964 onwards

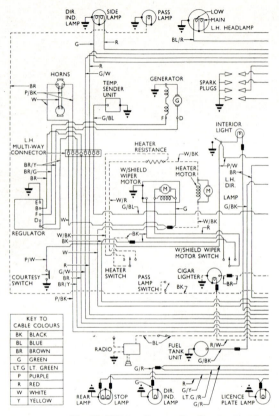

Fig. 48. Wiring diagram for Cortina Standard

KEY TO CABLE COLOURS	
BK	BLACK
BL	BLUE
BR	BROWN
G	GREEN
LT.G	LT. GREEN
P	PURPLE
R	RED
W	WHITE
Y	YELLOW

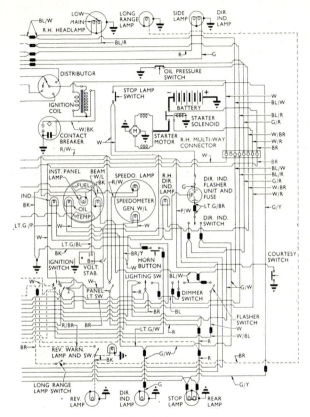

and de Luxe models, October 1964 onwards

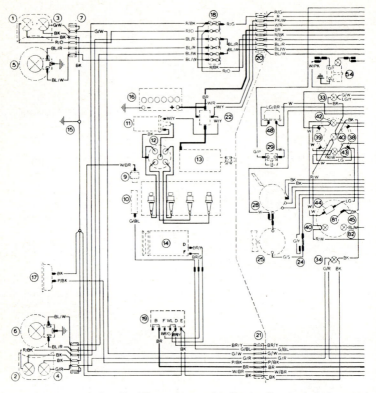

Fig. 49. Wiring diagram for Cortina Standard, de Luxe and

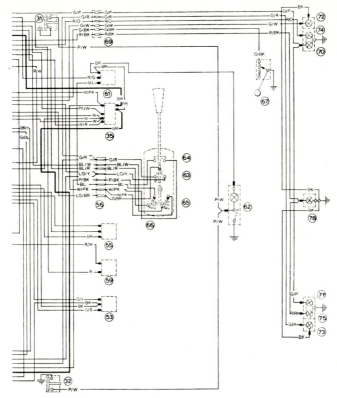

Super models, October 1967 onwards. (*For key see page* 108)

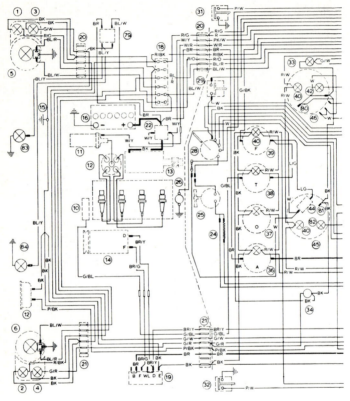

Fig. 50. Wiring diagram for Cortina, GT and 1600

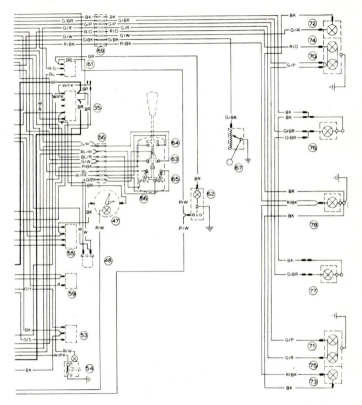

October 1967 onwards. (*For key see page* 108)

Key to Figs. 49 and 50

1. R.H. side lamp (front)
2. L.H. side lamp (front)
3. R.H. direction indicator (front)
4. L.H. direction indicator (front)
5. R.H. headlamp
6. L.H. headlamp
7. R.H. front loom connector
8. L.H. front loom connector
9. Oil pressure switch
10. Temperature gauge sender unit
11. Coil
12. Distributor
13. Starter motor
14. Generator
15. Body earth
16. Battery
17. Horn
18. Fuses
19. Regulator
20. R.H. bulkhead multi-way connector
21. L.H. bulkhead multi-way connector
22. Starter motor solenoid
24. Heater motor ballast resistor
25. Heater motor
26. Reversing lamp switch
28. Windscreen wiper motor
29. Stop lamp switch
31. R.H. courtesy light switch
32. L.H. courtesy light switch
33. R.H. indicator warning light
34. L.H. indicator warning light
35. Ignition switch
36. Ammeter (GT)
37. Oil-pressure gauge (GT)
38. Temperature gauge
39. Fuel gauge

40. Instrument lights
42. Generator warning light
43. Oil pressure warning light
44. Instrument voltage stabiliser
45. Speedometer
46. Tachometer (GT)
47. Electric clock (GT)
48. Flasher unit
53. Heater switch
54. Cigar lighter (where fitted)
55. Windscreen wiper switch
56. Steering column connector
59. Panel light switch
61. Lighting switch
62. Interior light
63. Direction indicator switch
64. Horn switch
65. Dip switch
66. Headlamp flasher switch
67. Fuel gauge sender unit
69. Rear wiring connector
70. R.H. stop lamp
71. L.H. stop lamp
72. R.H. direction indicator (rear)
73. L.H. direction indicator (rear)
74. R.H. rear light
75. L.H. rear light
76. R.H. reversing light (where fitted)
77. L.H. reversing light (where fitted)
78. Rear number plate light
79. Driving lamps relay (where fitted)
80. Tachometer earth (GT)
81. Speedometer earth
82. Main beam warning light
83. R.H. driving lamp (where fitted)
84. L.H. driving lamp (where fitted)

9 Steering, suspension and tyres

REGULAR lubrication of the steering gear on 1,340 c.c. models, at the intervals indicated in the maintenance schedule (Chapter 2), will prevent unnecessary friction, which will not only make the steering heavy and insensitive but will also lead to rapid wear of the joints in the linkage. On 1,500 c.c. and later cars the use of plastic bushes and "sealed-for-life" bearings eliminates the need for this attention but the steering gearbox will, of course, still require topping-up from time to time.

Satisfactory steering and tyre life depend not only on the condition of the steering gearbox and connexions but also on the maintenance of the correct "geometry," which can be upset as a result of a minor kerb collision. Because the castor, camber and swivel pin angles are determined by the initial assembly of the parts, accurate adjustment is beyond the scope of the owner.

First-class wheel alignment equipment is expensive and is therefore likely to be found only in the larger garages; but it does tend to reduce the margin of error that cannot entirely be ruled out when less efficient equipment is used. In addition to the alignment of the front wheels it allows three other important angles to be measured: castor, camber, and swivel-pin inclination. These are determined by the initial dimensions and assembly of the various parts of the front suspension. If they are upset by a minor accident or a kerb collision, a Ford dealer will be able to carry out the necessary checks to decide what replacements will be required.

When play develops in the self-adjusting joints in the steering linkage and thorough lubrication does not cure the trouble, new joints should be fitted. After a long period in service, wear will inevitably develop in the steering gearbox, although the recirculating-ball type of steering fitted has an exceptionally long life if it is properly lubricated. When slackness does develop, overhaul is a job for a Ford dealer. Not only is it necessary to remove the steering gearbox and column assembly from the car, but amateur attempts to service a vital component of this type may lead to serious trouble.

Similarly, on modern suspension systems the renewal of worn swivel pins or idler shafts and bushes is considered to be outside the scope of the average practical owner, although he may perhaps have tackled such work fairly successfully on a pre-war model.

The Suspension. The front wheels are independently sprung. At the rear, conventional semi-elliptic leaf springs are used. These, like the front springs, are damped by hydraulic shock absorbers.

Unfortunately the Cortina suffers from a trouble which has shown up on other cars fitted with MacPherson-strut front suspension—the danger of the upper mounting of the strut breaking away when rust develops in the wing around the strut mounting point. The cure is to have a rein-forcing plate welded over the rusted area. Your local Ford dealer should be able to carry out a completely satisfactory repair.

The rubber bushes used at various points in the suspension should not be lubricated, as oil or grease will cause rapid deterioration of the rubber. If they should develop squeaks or creaking noises, a little brake fluid (which is harmless to rubber) will usually silence them.

While carrying out these jobs the shock absorbers should be examined for any signs of leakage of fluid.

The Wheels. When the front wheels are jacked up for hub lubrication as described in Chapter 3, it is as well to take the opportunity of testing the bearings for wear by grasping the tyre at the top and bottom and rocking the wheel vertically about the hub. Do not confuse any possible looseness which may exist in the steering pivots with wheel bearing play: watch for relative movement between the brake disc or drum and the brake calliper or backplate.

If excessive play exists in the front wheel bearings or there is any sign of oil leakage into the brake drums, it is as well to seek the advice of a Ford dealer. For the do-it-yourself enthusiast, the method of lubricating and adjusting the hub bearings is described in Chapter 3.

Tyres. Apart from regular pressure checks (about which more will be said later), longer life can be obtained from a set of tyres by equalizing, as far as possible, the wear on the individual treads. This calls for changing the wheels around at 3,000-mile intervals. Fig. 51 shows alternative schemes, the choice depending on whether a reliable tyre is fitted to the spare wheel.

When radial-ply tyres are fitted, the steering and roadholding can be adversely affected if the interval between changing the tyres around is much greater than 3,000 miles, as the front and rear tyres quickly develop different tread profiles. Some experts claim, in fact, that there is little to be gained from swapping radial-ply tyres from front to rear, although changing the wheels from one side of the car to the other may help.

When rapid tread wear occurs on the front tyres, the alignment of the front wheels should be checked as recommended on page 109. An error of $\frac{1}{2}$ in. in alignment will have the same effect as dragging a spinning tyre sideways for nearly 90 ft in every mile on the road!

Incorrect camber angle and swivel-pin inclination will cause more rapid wear on one side of the tyre than the other; driving on steeply-cambered roads will have the same effect. An unbalanced wheel and tyre will cause a twisting, tramping action that will not only affect the steering and cause vibration, but will also grind rubber off the tyre tread and accelerate wear on the steering linkage and front suspension. Most larger garages, nowadays, have wheel-balancing equipment on which both static and dynamic balance can be checked and corrected quickly and at a

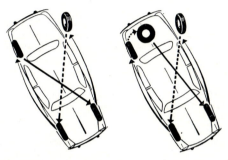

Fig. 51. Alternative methods of changing cross-ply tyres around to equalize tread wear

modest cost. This service is essential on the cars covered by this book, which are capable of maintaining high cruising speeds.

Unfortunately, it is also necessary to remember that speed costs money: tyres wear twice as quickly at 65 m.p.h. as at 35 m.p.h. and fast cornering, rapid acceleration and heavy braking must all be paid for in terms of tread rubber left on the road.

Pressure Checks. The tyre pressures should be checked only when the tyres are *cold*. Even a short run will warm-up the tyres and raise the pressures, thus giving a misleading reading on the gauge. Always use a good-quality tyre pressure gauge.

Whenever pressures are checked, make sure that the valve caps are replaced and tightened firmly. These are intended to prevent leakage and at the same time exclude mud, grit and ice from the relatively vulnerable inner seals. If a cap should be lost, fit a replacement as soon as possible.

10 Brake adjustment and servicing

GIRLING hydraulic brakes are fitted on all models. The pressure generated in a master cylinder when the brake pedal is depressed is transmitted
equally throughout the system to operating pistons in cylinders attached
to the brake backplates or incorporated in the callipers of the front
brakes. This ensures balanced braking—provided, of course, that the
brakes are correctly adjusted and that the effectiveness of one or more
of the brake linings is not reduced by oil or grease. The handbrake
operates the rear brake shoes by mechanical linkage.

Routine Maintenance. At 6,000-mile intervals check the level of the
fluid in the master cylinder reservoir, which should be kept about three-
quarters full; do not fill it to the brim. The brake reservoir is mounted,
with the similar clutch fluid reservoir, on the engine bulkhead near the
steering column.

It will be necessary to add fluid at regular intervals, owing to the automatic repositioning of the pistons in the front-wheel disc brakes to
compensate for friction lining wear; but a rapid fall in fluid level would
indicate a leak at some point in the system, which should be traced and
rectified. Use only the specified type of brake fluid.

The brake hoses should be checked at regular intervals for leakage,
chafing and general deterioration. They should in any case be renewed
after 36,000 miles or 3 years in service, and new rubber seals should be
fitted throughout the braking system at the same time. The old hydraulic
fluid should be pumped out and the system refilled with fresh fluid.

It is also advisable occasionally to check the tightness of the brake
mounting bolts and hydraulic unions. It is important not to overtighten
the bleed screws and unions, however, since this may very easily result in
stripped threads.

During the 6.000-mile service, or about twice a year, check the condition
of the brake linings. In the case of the rear brakes it will be necessary to
take off the drums—a simple job after removing the wheel and unscrewing
the drum retaining screw. If the linings are worn to such an extent that
the rivets are almost flush with the face of the friction material, the time
has come to fit new shoes, as described on pages 116–19. While the drums are
off, check the wheel cylinders for any signs of leakage of hydraulic fluid

past the seals and also make sure that there has been no seepage of oil from the hub bearing into the drum.

When drum brakes are fitted to the front wheels it will be necessary to remove the combined drum and front hub assemblies as detailed on pages 20–1, where the lubrication of the front hub bearings is described. The brake linings and operating cylinders—two cylinders to each wheel in this case—will then be accessible for a careful inspection of the amount of wear on the linings and for evidence of any leakage of fluid from the brake cylinders or of oil past the hub bearing oil seal.

Fig. 52. Rear brake with drum removed

This is typical of all models except the self-adjusting brake, on which no manual adjuster is fitted. At 5,000-mile intervals make sure that the rivets 1 are below the surface of the friction lining, 2. Check the adjuster 3 for binding and the pull-off springs 4 for effectiveness. Examine the expander 5 for signs of fluid leakage. See that the steady-springs 6 are correctly fitted

Where the front brakes are of the disc type, the amount of wear on the friction linings in the brake callipers can be checked when the wheel has been removed. If the thickness of the lining is reduced to about ⅛ in., new brake pads must be fitted, either by a Ford dealer or, if you tackle the job yourself, by following the method outlined on page 119. In no circumstances should the linings be allowed to wear down to a thickness of less than $\frac{1}{16}$ in.

Bleeding the Brakes. If the level of the fluid in the reservoir is allowed to fall too low—or if a pipeline union is disconnected or slackens off—air will enter the braking system. It will then be necessary to "bleed" the brakes.

A nipple that incorporates a valve will be found on each backplate or disc-brake calliper. If a rubber dust cap is fitted, remove this and attach a rubber or transparent plastic tube to one of the nipples, passing it through a box or ring spanner that fits the hexagon on the nipple. Submerge the free end of the tube in a little brake fluid in a clean glass jar. Open the bleeder screw one complete turn. Get an assistant to depress the brake pedal slowly and allow it to return unassisted. This pumping action should be repeated with a slight pause between each operation. Meanwhile, keep a watch on the flow of liquid into the jar and when air bubbles cease to appear, the pedal should be held down firmly and the bleeder screw securely tightened. Repeat this operation on all wheel cylinders, finishing at the wheel nearest to the master cylinder.

If your car is fitted with a dual-line braking system which provides separate hydraulic circuits for the front and rear brakes (usually fitted only to export models), have a word with your Ford dealer before attempting to bleed the brakes. If a valve and switch assembly is fitted in the system to give warning of failure of one of the circuits, it will be very difficult to persuade the warning light to go out and stay out unless the piston in the switch assembly is held in the central position with a special tool.

Flushing the System. After 24,000 miles or two years in service the system should be drained, flushed and refilled. To do this, pump all fluid out of the system through the bleeder screw of each wheel cylinder in turn, as described above, and discard it. Fill the reservoir with methylated spirit and flush the system by pumping as before. The supply tank should be replenished until at least a quart of spirit has passed through each wheel cylinder. Finally, pump the reservoir dry, refill with clean brake fluid and "bleed" the system.

Unfortunately, if the fluid has been contaminated by the use of mineral oil, all the hydraulic units, including the pipe-lines, should be dismantled and thoroughly cleaned and all rubber parts, including flexible hoses, should be replaced. If an oil has been used, this will frequently separate out when the fluid is allowed to stand in a glass jar; the layers of different fluid can then be seen. The contaminated fluid should be destroyed immediately to avoid it being accidentally re-used.

Brake Adjustment. Disc-type front brakes are self-adjusting; drum-type front brakes and the rear brakes, which are also of the drum type on all models, however, should be adjusted as described below except for the rear brakes on later models which, like the front disc brakes, are self-adjusting. Make this a routine check during the 6,000-mile service.

On each rear-brake backplate is a square-headed, screwed adjusting spindle, diametrically opposite to the mechanical expander mechanism operated by the handbrake cable.

Place chocks in front of and behind one of the front wheels to prevent the car from rolling, and release the handbrake. Jack up one rear wheel until it is free to rotate.

Turn the adjuster in a clockwise direction until solid resistance is felt. Then slacken it back until the brake drum can be rotated (usually two clicks). A slight drag may be felt from the trailing shoe but this should not be sufficient to prevent the wheel from being turned by hand.

Spin the wheel and apply the brakes hard to centralize the shoes in the drum and recheck the adjustment. When correctly adjusted there should be about ¼ in. free movement of the brake pedal pad before the plunger in the master cylinder begins to move.

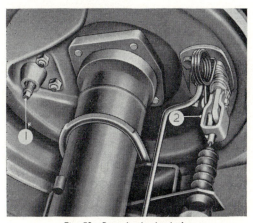

Fig. 53. Rear brake backplate
1. *Adjuster spindle.* 2. *Handbrake linkage*

Two square-headed adjusters are fitted to the backplate of each drum-type front brake. Adjustment is carried out in a similar manner to that just described for the rear brakes, each adjuster being turned clockwise until the drum is locked and then slackened back just sufficiently to obtain the minimum running clearance.

Any rubbing or scraping sound, or resistance to rotation of the wheel, calls for further investigation. First, however, make sure that the shoes are correctly centralized by spinning the wheel in the normal direction of rotation and again applying the foot-brake hard.

If this does not cure the trouble, light scraping noises may be due to nothing more serious than an accumulation of dust and grit in the drums. If the noise or friction occurs only at one point during the rotation of the wheel, a distorted drum may be suspected.

When Brakes Rub or Remain On. If noticeable friction is evident when the shoes have been correctly adjusted and backed-off as just described, the shoes are binding. Among likely causes are a broken or unhooked brake shoe return spring, swollen rubber seals on the shoe-operating piston, incorrectly adjusted handbrake cables or a seized lever in the rear brake operating cylinder.

If all the brakes should bind to approximately the same extent, the fluid reservoir may have been overfilled. If the level is correct, make sure that the air vent in the cap is not clogged. If these points are satisfactory, it is advisable to enlist the aid of a Ford dealer. Overhaul of the hydraulic components of the system is, strictly speaking, the province of the specialist.

Road-testing the Brakes. After adjustment the brakes should be tested on a dry-surfaced, preferably uncambered, road. Apply them hard at about 30 m.p.h. and examine the marks on the road to determine whether any wheel is locking before the remainder. It should also be noted whether there is a tendency to pull towards one side of the road.

If the brakes are inefficient or unbalanced, a likely cause is probably grease on the linings. The use of correct front wheel bearing lubricant and care not to overfill the back axle, as well as replacing grease retainers when leakage is indicated, will help to maintain braking efficiency. If the linings are badly saturated with grease or oil, new or relined brake shoes or friction pads should be fitted, as described in the following pages.

Handbrake Adjustment. Normally, adjustment of the rear brakes will automatically adjust the handbrake. It should not be necessary to disturb the adjustment of the primary cable which connects the handbrake lever to the equalizer on the rear-axle casing or the cable connecting the equalizer to the brakes, unless any parts have been renewed. Strictly speaking, this job is best left to a Ford dealer. The principle is to make sure that the rear brake operating levers are fully "off" and then to adjust the primary and secondary cables so that all slack is taken up, while ensuring that the brake operating levers and the equalizing lever have not been moved off their stops.

Relining the Brakes. Dismantling the rear brakes is quite straight-forward, but before removing the brake shoes it is as well to have handy some means of retaining the operating pistons in their cylinders. Other-wise, owing to the slight residual pressure that is maintained in the braking system, the pistons will tend to creep outwards, resulting in loss of fluid and entry of air into the system. Short lengths of wire or twine will serve, or better still, stout rubber bands cut from an old inner tube. Also, make a note of the way in which the pull-off springs are fitted to the shoes.

The backplate should be thoroughly cleaned with paraffin. If there is any evidence of leakage of oil or grease from the hub bearing, the oil seal must be renewed. Otherwise, the new lining will remain effective for only

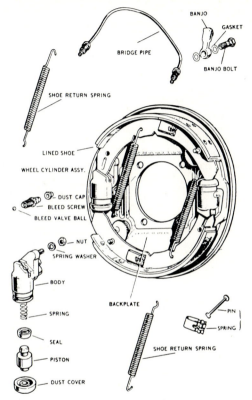

Fig. 54. Front drum brake fitted to earlier Cortina models

a short period. Similarly, it is seldom advisable to clean oil-soaked linings with petrol or paraffin in an attempt to obtain a further period of service.

It is also false economy to purchase cheap linings from a cut-price supplier, or to attempt to rivet new linings to the existing shoes without the use of an efficient lining clamp. The safest plan is to fit only factory-relined shoes.

The full benefit will not be obtained from new linings, of course, if the brake drums are badly scored. Unless the ridges are very deep, a specialist will be able to regrind the drums.

It is always a good plan to renew the pull-off springs when fitting replacement shoes, as weak springs can be a cause of brake judder or squeal. Some old hands recommend that the ends of the new linings should be bevelled-off, also with the object of preventing squeal or judder.

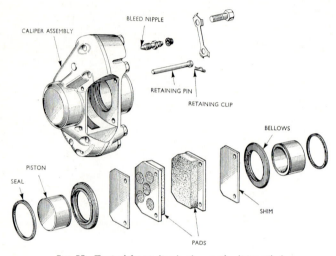

Fig. 55. Typical front disc brake partly dismantled

The method of removing the friction pads is clearly shown. The operating pistons, however, should not normally be disturbed. Shims may not be fitted to some earlier brakes

This, however, has been proved to be a complete fallacy—bevelling the leading edges of the linings, in fact, is often apt to cause or contribute to these troubles. The edges of the linings should be perfectly clean and square.

Dismantling Drum-type Brakes. To remove the shoes, jack up the car and remove a road wheel. Make sure that the handbrake is fully released. Slacken off all available adjustment by turning the adjuster anti-clockwise to the full extent.

Remove the countersunk screw securing the rear brake drum to the axle flange or hub and remove the brake drum. A light blow on the side of the drum will loosen it if it sticks. In the case of drum-type front brakes, remove the combined drum and hub assembly as described on pages 20–1.

Release the damper spring assemblies from the webs of the shoes by sliding the springs from beneath the peg heads. The pegs may then be withdrawn from the rear of the backplate.

The brake shoe linings are offset on the platforms to which they are attached. The end of the shoe at which the greater length of platform is exposed is known as the "toe" whilst the other end is termed the "heel." The leading and trailing shoes are identical.

Disengage one shoe from the locating slots in the wheel cylinder piston and abutment by pulling it against the tension of the pull-off springs. The other shoe will then automatically be released.

To refit the shoes, smear the shoe platforms with new brake grease but keep the linings clean. Lay the shoes on a bench with the toe of the leading shoe adjacent to the heel of the trailing shoe.

Connect the pull-off springs between the shoes as shown in the appropriate illustration. Both springs should be fitted to the outer sides of the brake shoe flanges.

Offer up the shoes, complete with pull-off springs, to the backplate and locate the leading shoe in the slots in the wheel cylinder piston and abutment. Prise the trailing shoe into position with its ends locating in the wheel cylinder body and abutment. Refit the damper spring assemblies.

Clean the brake drum, refit it and secure it with the setscrew. Refit the road wheel and adjust the brakes as described earlier. Immediately after fitting replacement shoes it is advisable to slacken back the adjuster one further click to allow for possible lining expansion, reverting to normal adjustment afterwards.

Several hard applications of the brake pedal should be made to ensure that all the parts are working satisfactorily and that the shoes are bedding to the drums. Finally, test the brakes on the road.

Renewing Disc Brake Pads. The friction linings of the front brakes are bonded and riveted to their pressure plates and can therefore be renewed only by fitting complete new brake pad assemblies. It should not be necessary to "bleed" the system after replacing the brake pads.

To remove the worn pads, jack up the front of the car and remove the road wheels. In each calliper there are two retaining pins which are held in place by two clips. Remove the clips and withdraw the pins. Using a screwdriver, lever the brake pads and the anti-squeal shims from their positions on either side of the disc.

Before fitting the new brake pads, the pistons should be pushed to the bottom of their cylinder bores. A simple method of doing this is to open the bleed screw one turn, at the same time pushing the pistons inwards, thus allowing a small amount of fluid to escape.

Place the pads and shims in position and refit the retaining pins and clips. Pump the brake pedal until solid resistance is felt and top-up the master cylinder reservoir with clean brake fluid.

Brake Servo Unit. On the disc-braked Corsair and G.T. models, servo assistance is provided by a vacuum cylinder, connected to the induction manifold, which increases the fluid pressure in the brake pipe-line in proportion to the amount of effort applied by the driver to the brake pedal.

Servo units normally have very long, trouble-free lives and when trouble does crop up, the usual practice is to exchange the faulty unit for a works-reconditioned servo. Special tools are needed to dismantle, assemble and test the servo, so inexpert tinkering is not to be recommended.

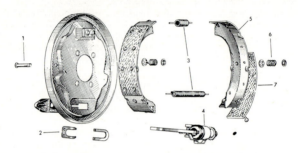

Fig. 56. Self-adjusting rear brake assembly

1. Shoe steady pin
2. Expander retaining clips
3. Pull-off springs
4. Expander housing with automatic adjuster
5. Brake shoe
6. Shoe steady spring
7. Friction lining

The only attention required in normal service is to change the air filter whenever the front disc brake pads are renewed. The servo is mounted in an easily accessible position in the engine compartment and the filter cover is retained by a simple wire clip. After the new element has been installed, check the tightness of the clips on the brake vacuum hose and see that the hose does not show any signs of collapsing or perishing. Also check the hydraulic pipeline unions on the servo for any signs of seepage of brake fluid.

Index